J. A. Hobson

J. A. Hobson

Jules Townshend

LIVERPOOL
UNIVERSITY
LIBRARY

FIAT LVX

Manchester University Press
Manchester and New York

Distributed exclusively in the USA and Canada by St. Martin's Press, New York

Copyright © Jules Townshend 1990

Published by Manchester University Press,
Oxford Road, Manchester, M13 9PL, UK
and Room 400, 175 Fifth Avenue, New York, NY 10010, USA

Distributed exclusively in the USA and Canada
by St. Martin's Press, Inc., 175 Fifth Avenue, New York, NY 10010, USA

British Library cataloguing in publication data
Townshend, Jules
  J. A. Hobson. — (Lives of the left)
  1. Economics. Hobson, J. A.
  I. Title   II. Series
  330.092

Library of Congress cataloging in publication data
Townshend, Jules, 1945–
     J. A. Hobson / Jules Townshend.
        p. cm.
     Includes bibliographical references.
     ISBN 0-7190-2184-7
     1. Hobson, J. A. (John Atkinson), 1858-1940.
  2. Economics – Great Britian – Biography. I. Title
  HB103.H55T68   1990
  330.15'5 – dc20   90-6433

ISBN 0 7190 2184 7 *hardback*

Set in Perpetua
by Koinonia Ltd, Manchester

Printed in Great Britain
by Biddles Ltd, Guildford and Kings Lynn

Contents

To Bobby and in memory of Eva

Preface

My prefatory remarks can be encapsulated in two paradoxes. The first is that the purpose of this work is ambitious, yet at the same time modest. It presents a fresh interpetation of Hobson that challenges existing ones. Several of things are attempted: first, to demonstrate how he was a systematic thinker, whatever his personal disclaimers; secondly, to situate his thinking within the 'crisis' of late nineteenth-century British liberalism and to show how he tried to embed his theory within social and political practices; and finally, I seek to assess the coherence of his 'system'. Nevertheless, this offering is made with some humility, made in the knowledge that in academic terms the Hobson 'seam' has not been fully mined, and that the law of diminishing returns has not yet set in. Hobson's published literary output was phenomenal, both in quantity and diversity. This makes an evaluation of the totality of his thought difficult in an age of intense academic specialisation both within and between disciplines. Moreover, the compass of this book prevents a detailed account of all his intellectual and political concerns, and of how certain ideas and attitudes changed over time. In addition, a more precise scrutiny of his intellectual influences is required, given his notorious coyness in acknowledging his intellectual debts.

As for my own debts, we can take note of Hobson's remark that production in the modern age is pre-eminently social in character. This work is no less so. Since its first apperance as a Ph.D. thesis, significant commentaries on Hobson have been published. I have learnt a good deal from John Allett, Peter Cain and Michael

Freeden, whatever my reservations. In particular, I have become more sensitised to the issues and themes contained in the Hobson writings. I also wish to thank David Howell and Raymond Plant for their suggested improvements to the original manuscript, as well as my colleagues at Manchester Polytechnic, especially Phil Mole and Keith Gibbard. All have been generous with their time in a period when the pressure to increase academic and pedagogic productivity has become great. The person I thank most is my 'partner' Maureen, some of whose analytical acumen has hopefully rubbed off on me over the years.

And here we come to the second paradox. Whilst Hobson may have been correct in judging production to be social, he forgot to add that intellectual production is abidingly anti-social, full of emotional and practical opportunity costs. Maureen, Rachel, Matthew and Saoirse have all in their different ways reminded me that the meaning of life does not lie in the study.

Jules Townshend

1 Life and project

Reputation is something over which the individual is powerless. In life our peers or the 'public' decide. In death it becomes the property of posterity. We have no right of appeal. Invariably significance is attributed to something that is not part of the individual's prime intention. Such is the reputation of John Atkinson Hobson. He is well known as a forerunner of the 'Keynesian revolution' to historians of economic thought, as an important theorist of economic reformism within the British labour movement to labour historians, as precursor to Lenin's theory of imperialism to historians of Marxism and as one of the theoretical architects of the British welfare state to historians of social administration. Yet such a reputation distorts the thrust and scope of his political and intellectual activities. Indeed, he has become a victim of what he vehemently criticised: academicism with its excessive and exclusive specialisation, and its ostensible moral indifference. He would have accused posterity of the crime of compartmentalisation and its failure to recognise his unified or interdisciplinary approach to understanding society and its problems in all its interconnected dimensions. As G. D. H. Cole noted on the centenary of Hobson's birth: 'I prefer to think of him chiefly, as he thought of himself, as the champion of a comprehensive study of the conditions of human welfare embracing all the social studies, within which economic and other specialist subjects were really no more than subordinate and closely interrelated branches.'[1]

He could have complained that even *this* appreciation of his thought missed his political purpose. Social analysis was a guide to action. Social facts and theories had an intrinsic moral import. Hobson saw himself simultaneously as an observer of, and an active agent in, the world of politics, as well as uniting a theory and practice of social reform. He wrote in his earliest work on social philosophy: 'a Social Question which is left to professed philosophers can never be answered. A satisfactory answer cannot consist in the theoretic solution of a problem; it must lie in the region of social conduct.'[2]

The trajectory and character of his intellectual and political preoccupations throughout his life were formed by his attempt to answer one question: how to solve the 'crisis' of late nineteenth-century liberalism ? Whilst the term the 'crisis of liberalism' was used somewhat later by Hobson as a title for a book published in 1909, he was merely reiterating a perspective he had developed a decade earlier. Hobson and other 'progressives' perceived the 'crisis' as two fold, as a crisis of the Liberal Party, and of liberal philosophy. Naturally, Hobson, the intellectual, saw the party's crisis as a result of intellectual failure. It no longer represented a plausible, coherent and attractive set of ideas that had kept abreast with the modern world. Its guiding doctrine of a minimal state, as expressed in *laissez-faire* and its counterpart in foreign affairs, non-intervention – even if principles not always strictly adhered to in practice – were increasingly questioned by new intellectual trends and political forces: imperialists, socialists and a multitude of single-issue, social reformers. The demand to widen or change the scope of state action was indelibly etched on the political agenda. What Hobson sought to do was 'modernise' liberal theory and thereby revitalise the Liberal Party, or, alternatively, bring into being a new coalition of political forces that would realise his profoundly modified liberal principles. His aim was to rejuvenate liberalism as a hegemonic force within British politics. For Hobson, this involved the fusion of liberal and socialist values and concepts.

The task he set himself in remodelling liberal theory was on a grand scale. It entailed a synthesis of many different disciplines within the human sciences – economics, ethics, sociology, political sociology, political philosophy, psychology, social psychology and biology – at a time when the academic world was becoming increasingly specialised. Indeed, Hobson's significance within the history of liberalism lies precisely in this: along with his friend L. T. Hobhouse, he was one of the last liberals to work within such a holistic perspective. Although liberalism is still of great political and intellectual significance in the modern world, it is far more fragmented, and less systematic, than Hobson would have wanted.[3]

A heretic's life

There was little in Hobson's background to suggest that he would become an 'economic heretic', as he described himself. He wrote in his autobiography: 'Born and bred in the middle stratum of the middle class of a middle-sized industrial town of the Midlands, I was favourably situated for a complacent acceptance of the existing social order.'[4] He was born in 1858, into a respectable, upper middle-class family from Derby. He was the second eldest of four children in this family. His eldest brother, Ernest William (1856-1933), became a Professor in Mathematics at Cambridge. His father, William Hobson, a devout low churchman, was a founder and proprietor of the *Derbyshire and North Staffordshire Advertiser*. Active as a Liberal in local politics, he was town mayor on two occasions. John was educated at the local grammar school, where he eventually became head-boy. The explanation for his heretical outlook seems to lie in his intellectual disposition – a fearless and ruthless questioning of commonly held beliefs and attitudes, and a preparedness to follow wherever his intellect took him. Thus, theological reflection had by early manhood led him to abandon orthodox Christianity and embrace a form of humanism. This humanism was reinforced by his studies at Oxford University – he had won a classical scholarship to Lincoln College in 1876.[5]

His heretic's fate, however, was well and truly sealed somewhat later. After Oxford he settled down to a quiet life of teaching, first at Faversham and then at Exeter. In this period he married Florence Edgar, daughter of a New York attorney, initiating a lifelong connection with the United States. Indeed, his writings have been more respected in that country than in his own. He went there on many occasions and became friendly, or acquainted, with many leading progressive American intellectuals, such as H. D. Lloyd, Thorsten Veblen, Edward Ross, R. T. Ely and W. C. Mitchell. His radicalisation began in earnest when he moved to London in 1887. He gave up schoolmastering for journalism and university extension work. He was tempted into heresy by A. F. Mummery, a businessman and famous mountaineer. Under his influence, he helped Mummery write *The Physiology of Industry* (1889), which challenged the prevailing view that capitalism was a self-equilibriating system. They argued that depressions were inherent because oversaving was inevitable, causing a lack of demand for current output. They scandalised academic orthodoxy, not only by suggesting that *laissez-faire* capitalism was fatally flawed but also by criticising the Protestant thrift ethic. Whilst Keynes later noted that this book marked 'an epoch in economic thought',[6] it also marked the beginning of a long epoch in Hobson's life. He was barred from giving extension lectures in Political Economy at the University of London, and an invitation to deliver lectures on economics on behalf of the Charity Organisation Society was mysteriously withdrawn. So began, unwittingly, his long ambivalent relationship with academic orthodoxy. He wanted academic recognition, but this was denied him.[7] His underconsumptionism, his mixing of ethical belief with scientific commitment, his looseness of thought, his interdisciplinary approach at a time when academics were increasingly becoming more specialised, and his constant accusation that the academic fraternity was not above class partisanship, put him beyond the pale. He regretted the fact that his life of journalism had led him to be less intellectually rigorous than he would have liked. Yet, if he had been admitted into academia, he may have become, for posterity at least, a far less interesting figure. He may have become less politically active, and his radicalism more tempered. He may also have been compelled to specialise, thereby losing the intellectual breadth, so characteristic of his thought and one of its most engaging facets.

His membership of two intellectual groupings, the Ethical Movement and the Rainbow Circle, strengthened his radicalism. For six years he was a member of the London Ethical Society, an organisation founded by followers of T. H. Green, who rejected Christianity but needed a surrogate religion. It was here that he met William Clarke, who brought him into contact with Fabian and American progressive ideas, and who also developed in Hobson a strong antipathy to imperialism. In 1896 he left the the London Ethical Society, because of its highly individualistic approach to social amelioration, and joined the South Place Ethical Society, which was far more collectivist in orientation. He became one of its permanent lecturers in 1899, a post he held until shortly before his death. Members of the Society, at one time or another, included Gilbert Murray, Herbert Burrows, L. T. Hobhouse, Bertrand Russell, John Robertson, Graham Wallas, Norman Angell, H. Bradlaugh Bonner, Patrick Geddes and G. Lowes Dickinson.

Hobson in addition belonged to the Rainbow Circle, of which he was a founder member. The Circle, established in 1894, met for the next thirty years. It derived its name from its early venue, the Rainbow Tavern in Fleet Street. It was composed of liberal, socialist and Marxist intellectuals, journalists, civil servants and politicians. They were concerned primarily with developing a consensus amongst themselves on the question of widening the state's economic and social functions. Members included Ramsay MacDonald, Herbert Burrows, William Pember Reeves, Richard

Stapley, John Robertson, William Clarke, Murray MacDonald, Herbert Samuel, Percy Alden, Charles Trevelyan, Sydney Olivier, G. P. Gooch, Russell Rea, Francis Hirst, Edward Pease, J. L. Hammond, W. M. Crook and the Reverend H. C. Shuttleworth. Many of them played an important part in bringing about the 1906-14 Liberal reforms.[8]

His robust moral convictions were clearly evident during the Boer War (1899-1902). He had been sent out to South Africa by the *Manchester Guardian* as a special correspondent, just before the war broke out. His first-hand knowledge of the issues and underlying forces involved in the conflict brought him, on his return, to the fore in the so-called 'Little Englander' or 'pro-Boer' agitation against the war. Although physically frail, he addressed anti-war meetings, which were often broken up by jingoist thugs. From this period onwards Hobson became an ardent peace campaigner, opposing the arms build-up that culminated in the First World War. He helped to establish the British Neutrality Committee in 1914 (later called the Bryce Committee) to keep Britain out of the war. During and after the First World War he was also active in the Union of Democratic Control, the National Peace Council, the League for Peace and Freedom and the League of Nations Society. He also joined the 1917 Club in support of the first, February, Revolution in Russia. His continuing interest in international affairs was also demonstrated after the war. He agitated for a repeal of the reparations clauses of the Treaty of Versailles, and later he was a member of an Independent Labour Party (ILP) advisory committee on international questions, although he did not join the party itself.

Yet his main interest lay in domestic politics, although he continually stressed their dependency upon international factors. From the 1890s onwards he saw himself as part of a 'progressive movement', as reflected in his membership of the Rainbow Circle and the South Place Ethical Society, both of which politically and intellectually transcended party, and indeed, class, affiliations. Although he remained in the ranks of the Liberal Party until 1916 – the final straw for Hobson was its lurch towards protectionism – he was never an uncritical member. In a sense his approach was instrumental: his evaluation of the party depended upon its inclination and capacity to realise his 'progressive' ideas. In strategic terms, Hobson attempted throughout his political life to bring about an alliance between 'progressive' sections of the middle class and the organised working class. Indeed, this approach to party politics made it easier for him to join the Labour Party in 1924, after having unsuccessfully stood as an independent candidate in the 1918 elections. The Labour Party rather than the Liberal Party now seemed the organisation which would bring this alliance to fruition. Nevertheless, there was something semi-detached about his commitment to the Labour Party. He disliked its full-blooded socialists and its trade unionists who put the interests of class before the liberal ideal of community. Just as he had been part of a progressive pressure group within the Liberal Party, through his membership of the Rainbow Circle and later through the *Nation*, so within the Labour Party he worked with the ILP on international issues. More significantly, he formulated an ILP document with Brailsford, Creech Jones and E. F. Wise entitled *The Living Wage*. It contained his underconsumptionist analysis and was hotly debated at the 1927 Labour Party conference, but eventually became lost in a joint party/TUC Committee.

Hobson not only wanted to influence party policy, whether Liberal or Labour, he also tried to effect reform outside the orbit of both parties. In 1916 he served as a member of the Whitley Committee, which was later made into a sub-committee on industrial relations of the Ministry of Reconstruction. In addition he was appointed to its sub-committee on trusts. In 1919 he submitted evidence to the Sankey Coal Commission and appeared as a witness to the Colwyn Committee on National Debt and

Taxation. In 1929 he acted as official adviser – with little effect – to the government in attending the Prime Minister's (Ramsay Macdonald's) Conference on the Industrial Situation, set up to discover the best method of promoting industrial recovery.

Although economic reform was Hobson's central priority, his breadth of perspective and interest is revealed by his membership of various voluntary bodies, possibly facilitated by the fact that he had a small private income after his father's death in 1897. He was active on the Executive Committee of the Secular Education League, established in 1907. He was a founding member of the Sociological Society in 1904, its chairman (1913–22) and its vice-president (1922–32). Before the First World War he joined the Webbs on the National Committee for the Abolition of the Poor Law, and in 1914 was a member of the National Birth Rate Committee, whose purpose was to investigate the supposed failure of fertility in the British population.

Nevertheless, most of Hobson's time as a social reformer was devoted to theorising and propagandising. His palpable physical frailty belied his prodigious literary energy. He suffered from numerous bouts of insomnia and neuritis (inflammation of the nerves) and 'recognised that his constant appearance of ill-health did correspond to a real fact'.[9] H. W. Nevinson wrote: 'I suppose that for forty years at least the stupifying sword of death has been hanging over him by a cobweb', and speculated: 'Is it that unmoving peril which has driven him to produce more work and finer work than almost any healthy person I have known?'[10] He wrote over forty books, and published more than 600 reviews and articles on a huge variety of economic, political and literary topics. In the last decade of his life – he died in 1940 – whilst in his seventies, he produced nine books and over a hundred reviews and articles.

Appearances concealed something else. His intellectual and moral earnestness in print disguised the fact that he was something of a wit. He was known as the 'jester-in-chief' at the famous *Nation* lunches.[11] His wit, however, was never without bite. Thus, in commenting upon the anti-intellectualism of the English, he remarked: 'When an Englishman thinks, he thinks he is sick.'[12] His 'formidable gift for irony and satire'[13] only occasionally surfaced in print. His book *1920: Dips into the Near Future* (1918) contains many striking parallels with Orwell's *Nineteen Eighty-Four*.

In order to understand the intellectual rationale for all these practical, propagandising and literary activities, the contextual backdrop of his formative years in the 1890s, when he came to live in London, requires exploration. In this decade both liberal theory, and the Liberal Party were in 'crisis'. All Hobson's political and theoretical concerns in this period and subsequently were shaped by this experience.

The Liberal Party in crisis

Although the Liberal Party's fortunes revived in the 1906 general election, during the 1890s it was in deep trouble, virtually at every level.[14] Gladstone's departure as leader in 1894 was succeeded by the feuding duo of Lord Rosebery and Sir William Harcourt, who went as far as fighting the 1895 elections on separate platforms. Gladstone's departure also unleashed the latent centrifugal tendencies within the lower echelons of the Liberal Party, which often tended to put their particular interests and 'fads' above those of party: the Scots, the Irish, the Welsh, old-style radicals, new-style social reformers, education and temperance reformers, disestablishmentarians, imperialists and anti-imperialists. Already the party had been badly bruised in 1886 over the question of Irish Home Rule. A sizeable 'Whig' section defected, along with a smaller Radical group, led by the charismatic Joseph Chamberlain. Moreover, the party's electoral base began to shrink dramatically. The middle classes voted Tory in larger numbers, and the party came increasingly to rely on the 'Celtic' fringe of Wales and

Scotland at a time when the franchise had been widened to include many agricultural labourers and when the working class in industrial conurbations had become electorally significant as a result of boundary changes.

Indeed, the question of how to gain the support of the urban proletariat became, for Hobson, *the* question that the party had to confront head-on. As he wrote in his weekly column of his father's newspaper: '...the voting power is more and more with the working class'.[15] He and other Liberals believed – perhaps too simplistically – that vital lessons could be learnt from the Continent, where the German and Belgian Liberal Parties had been eclipsed by working-class, socialist parties. To avoid a similar fate, Hobson and his co-thinkers believed first, that the party had to co-operate with 'labour' to head-off the possibility of a successful, independent workers' party. They saw this as a realistic project as a result of similar collaboration in the form of a 'Progressive Party' on the London County Council that had been established in 1888. Both in order to co-operate with labour and attract the working-class electorate, they insisted that the party had to face up to two questions. The first was the so-called 'Social Problem'. The well-documented researches by Charles Booth and the new breed of middle-class social reformers in the 1880s revealed just how deep and widespread was urban poverty. Moreover, the persistence of the 'Great Depression', that had begun in 1873, strongly challenged the liberal faith in the benefits of *laissez-faire*. Liberals from the mid-nineteenth century onwards had assumed that capitalism, if left to itself, would smoothly expand, bringing prosperity to ever wider sections of the population.

Secondly, Hobson felt that, if the Liberal Party was going to have a future, it must address itself to working-class aspirations. These included greater parliamentary representation (through the party's adoption of working-class candidates), shorter working hours and reduced unemployment, all of which, if left unattended, could be exploited by socialist rivals. The London riots of 1886 and 1887, and the growth of 'new unionism' after the 1889 London dock strike, gave these issues a greater urgency. Hobson initially blamed Gladstone for the absence of a coherent, state-directed social policy. He attacked him for his obsession with Irish Home Rule – his 'pet hobby horse that he has ridden for so long'[16] – which prevented the possibility of implementing social legislation. 'He has completely played round the Eight Hours Day and other labour questions....'[17] 'During a political career of nearly sixty years, Mr Gladstone has carefully avoided facing these fundamental economic questions which form the true bedrock of politics...What has he ever suggested to redress this fundamental social grievance [i.e. social injustice]? Nothing.'[18] Thus, Hobson had correctly noted that Gladstone had effectively kept class issues out of politics. His moralistic approach had often led him to highlight questions of foreign policy. On the domestic front, social issues for Gladstone were at bottom moral ones, as they were for the party's middle-class Nonconformist rank and file. The solution to social problems lay in self-help, education and temperance, and did not warrant breaches in *laissez-faire* principles, or 'constructions' as he called them. Indeed, mainstream Liberal opinion can be summed up in a comment by John Morley, the leading Liberal spokesman on social affairs between 1887 and 1892 (and who later became a friend of Hobson's): '... a reform that would probably be worth all the other social reforms put together would be an improvement in the habits of the people in respect to temperance'.[19]

True, there were signs in the 1880s and early 1890s that certain sections of the Liberal Party were becoming more flexible on the question of *laissez-faire*, but only in relation to land questions, reflecting the Liberals' traditional antipathy to landowners. Thus, a piece of land legislation in the early 1880s interfered with the rights of land ownership in Ireland. And the so-called 'Unauthorised' Programme of 1885, designed to woo the newly enfranchised agricultural labourer, promised free land. At the parliamentary level, in the late 1880s, there emerged a grouping within the Liberal Party, which became known as the 'Liberal Imperialists' – Haldane, Grey, Fowler and Buxton – who intellectually embraced certain collectivist principles but had no specific policies in mind. Finally, the 1891 Newcastle Programme, the party's first official programme, made some vague refences to employers' liability and shortening of working hours. Yet, its main concern was with Irish Home Rule and Welsh Disestablishment.[20]

The party's refusal to consider seriously any collectivist principles was amply confirmed during its 1892-95 adminstration. Gladstone remained obsessed with Home Rule and, although the issue of old age pensions assumed increasing saliency, the Liberal-sponsored Royal Commission on the Aged Poor rejected a state-run scheme. In classic *laissez-faire* terms, it stated, 'Pauperism is becoming a constantly diminishing evil, ultimately to disappear before the continuous progress of thrift and social well-being'.[21]

The Liberal government failed to pass any litmus tests in demonstrating its responsiveness to well-established working-class demands. For instance, on the issue of the eight hour day, it argued that this was not something that the state could impose. It was for the trade unions themselves to attain. As for working-class representation in Parliament, it agreed in principle with payment of MPs, but did nothing in practice. Perhaps more damagingly for party prospects, local Liberal caucuses rejected working class candidates. On unemployment, the government declared that the finding of work was not a government responsibility.

The Liberals' cataclysmic defeat at the polls in 1895 was in Hobson's eyes conclusive proof that it had failed to consider seriously the 'Social Problem' and the working class's social and political aspirations. He supported a manifesto of sixteen Radical MPs which stated: 'The Liberal Party of the future should cease to base its policy upon the propaganda of middle class political organisation, and seek to secure the sympathy of the working classes by the active promotion of those land, labour and social reforms in which they are profoundly interested.[22] This failure to 'secure the sympathy of the working classes' was also attributed by Hobson to the party's social composition, especially the domination of the local Liberal caucuses by the middle and upper middle classes, who were hostile to labour's cause, greater Lib-Lab co-operation and the widening of working-class representation within the party.[23] Consequently, Hobson favoured the 'shedding' of these 'money-bags' as he dubbed them.

To tackle effectively the Social Problem one further obstacle had to be overcome – imperialism – a question over which the Party became increasingly divided as the century drew to a close. Hobson did not believe, as the Liberal imperialists claimed, that domestic reform and an active imperialist policy could be pursued simultaneously. Imperial expansion and war like posturing diverted political energies and economic resources away from remedying social problems, and strengthened the forces of reaction.

The intellectual crisis

Central to Hobson's strategy for the reorientation and future success of the Liberal Party – if it was to survive as a hegemonic force within British politics – was the need to convert it to 'progressive' principles.[24] If this were achieved, Hobson thought, the party's pressing political problems could be effectively resolved: the need to overcome the fissiparous forces threatening to pull the party apart, to give the working class greater confidence in the party's commitment to social reform and to attract working-class membership to the party, thereby averting the potential socialist threat that he saw from the fledgling ILP.[25] The Party had not only to jettison its 'money-bags' but also its outdated political philosophy and policies associated with the Benthamite and

Manchester Schools, that is, utilitarianism and *laissez-faire*. As the 'Introductory' to the ill-fated *Progressive Review*, organ of the Rainbow Circle (and of which Hobson was the assistant editor) asserted:

> The Benthamite philosophy and the economics of the Manchester School which gave certain theoretic basis and harmony to [the Liberal Party's] past career will not enable it to carry to completion the task of securing genuine economic freedom, still less to undertake the concerns and multifarious duties which devolve upon a modern state in contributing, by legislative and administrative acts, to secure the material and moral welfare of the people.[26]

Hobson firmly believed that traditional liberal philosophy required a complete overhaul if the Liberal Party was to survive. This necessitated a thorough criticism of the classical postulates not only in the light of changing political and economic circumstances but also as a result of the new intellectual climate: the emergence of novel ideas about human beings and their social world that had given rise to new notions of freedom, and challenged the traditional liberal conception.

Classical liberalism: Bentham and the Manchester School

Despite its extreme amorphousness, the liberal tradition, has been centrally preoccupied with the question of individual liberty. From this arose a number of large and complex questions: What were the basic ingredients of this liberty? What theory of human nature determined these ingredients? By what means should liberty be achieved? In particular, what should be the role and shape of the state in this process?

The utilitarian answer to the last question – the most significant one for Hobson – as interpreted by the Manchester School, whose leading apostle was Richard Cobden, lay in the idea of the 'umpire', or 'ring-holder' state or what in contemporary parlance is known as the 'minimal state'. The state's job was solely concerned with protecting life, liberty and property. Especially in the economic realm, it should be as non-interventionist as possible, pursuing a policy of '*laissez-faire*'. This minimalist doctrine rested upon a clearly articulated model of human nature which was developed by Jeremy Bentham and James Mill, the founders of the utilitarian movement in the late eighteenth and early nineteenth centuries. They regarded human beings as essentially self-regarding, pleasure-loving creatures, who naturally sought to avoid pain. What counted as pleasure and pain was up to the individual to determine: 'push-pin', according to Bentham, for one individual could be as good as poetry for another. Freedom meant the ability to pursue these hedonistic desires without interference from others.

That the state should have minimal functions rested on two arguments. First, since individual happiness was the overriding value, and s/he knew how best to achieve it, the state could not possess superior knowledge in this area of human conduct. Welfare was synonymous with the satisfaction of individual desires, not with achieving what might be desirable according to some other criterion, such as individual or communal needs, which could run counter to what a person may actually want. A paternalist (or 'nanny') state could not, and therefore should not, decide how an individual's welfare ought to be constituted. That was a private matter. There could be no legislating for taste.

The second argument rested on the assumption that a free market was the best – either ideally, or the best available – mechanism for promoting individual welfare. The utilitarians and the Manchester School derived their economic thinking from Adam Smith, although he was not nearly as rigidly non-interventionist as his disciples such as Cobden.[27] He maintained that the most efficacious and just way to maximise pleasures and increase the objects of consumption was through a market system. This not only ensured that people produced what others wanted – within the limits of their pockets – but that output was continually increased through a widening division of labour that enhanced productivity. The market also had the providential virtue of harnessing the activities of self-regarding individuals to work in the interests of others. Smith argued that if each person was allowed to 'study his own advantage', it would lead him 'to prefer that employment which is most advantageous to society'.[28] The market ensured that there was a 'natural' identification of interest between people. And what the producer – either worker or capitalist – got as a reward could be justified either on the grounds of efficiency or fairness. For example, a low wage indicated either that the worker was not producing what others wanted, or that s/he was not working hard enough. The job of the state, therefore, within the economic sphere was merely to ensure that contracts were kept and property protected.

The utilitarians and the classical economists also advanced a methodological defence of *laisssez-faire*. The economic system worked best when it operated according to a system of natural laws, with which the state should not tamper. Or, as Ricardo suggested, wages were distributed according to an 'iron law'. To pay workers above this law would be self-defeating, because it merely increased the population, and hence the supply of workers, thereby bringing down the price of labour to its original position.

Economics was indeed a 'dismal' science, especially for the poor. Richard Cobden put the matter graphically: 'They [the poor] might as well attempt to regulate the tide by force, or change the course of the seasons, or subvert any of the other laws of nature – for the wages of labour depend upon laws as unnerring and as much above our coercive power as any other operations of nature.'[29] Thus, the state could not interfere in order to improve the economic welfare of workers. And on moral grounds it should not attempt to do so either. In a letter to a friend, Cobden wrote in 1836 that he did not believe in that 'spurious humanity which would indulge in an unreasoning kind of philanthropy at the expense of the community. Mine is that masculine species of charity which leads me to inculcate in the minds of the labouring classes the love of independence, the privilege of self-respect, the disdain of being patronised or petted, the desire to accumulate, the ambition to rise.'[30] Such a perspective was part of his rigid *laissez-faire* doctrine, which sought to cut down governmental expense, bureaucracy and taxation. Nevertheless, in common with many other nineteenth-century liberals, he believed that education was a collective good. The civilising benefits it would bring to the 'lower orders' were too important to be left to private initiative.

The utilitarian view of human nature and *laissez-faire* doctrine had important implications for the theory of democracy and citizenship. Since everyone was egoistic, no one could be trusted. Thus, individuals required democratic rights to ensure that their rulers were accountable. Democracy, therefore, was conceived as a form of self-protection, and as such, it meant that the demands of citizenship were slight. The citizen merely had to check that the state was doing its job in protecting the private rights of life, liberty and property. The citizen was seen as essentially passive in the public sphere, and active in the private sphere. The 'good' citizen merely had to be law-abiding and check that the state fairly held the 'ring' to enable him or her to pursue actively their own self-interest. This individualistic conception of democracy posited a fundamental symmetry between the essentially politically passive citizen and the passive state. The latter ultimately had no directive role, merely an umpiring function of ensuring 'fair play', once it had secured the conditions of free competition. And the citizen's job was to check that it was properly fulfilling this function.

Democracy was not, therefore, to be explained or justified as, for example, a manifestation of a human being's social nature, a desire to participate in a communal life, or to involve him or herself in decisions that were beneficial in the first instance to society as a whole. Indeed, this minimalist perspective saw the common good as merely the aggregation of self-interests and satisfactions of individuals seen in isolation from each other. There was no common interest that transcended this private aggregation.

Classical liberalism challenged: J. S. Mill, T. H. Green and H. Spencer

Hobson and his *Progressive Review* colleagues were not the first to question classical liberalism from within the tradition itself, either methodologically or as a set of explanatory principles and political prescriptions. By the time Hobson arrived on the intellectual scene in the late 1880s, the classical mould had been irrevocably fractured in a variety of ways by the three intellectual giants of mid- and late-Victorian liberalism: Mill, Green and Spencer.

J. S. Mill

Mill rejected the egoistic, hedonistic account of human nature offered by his father, James Mill, and Bentham. He distinguished between lower and higher pleasures, which roughly corresponded to pleasures of the body and mind (which included the pursuit of wisdom and altruistic action). Individuals who experienced both pleasures would confirm that those of the mind were indeed higher. Hence, 'push-pin' was no longer as good as poetry. It was better to be 'Socrates dissatisfied than a pig satisfied', said Mill. Human beings had an intrinsically moral potential that transcended self-interest. This created the possibility for them to become socially responsible citizens. Thus, he introduced a qualitative dimension into the Benthamite calculus, something, as we shall see, that Hobson also did in his 'New Utilitarianism.'

Nevertheless, Mill was broadly committed to *laissez-faire* in the economic sphere, and consequently to the view that the state had no special responsibility in looking after the material welfare of the mass of the population. The possibility of an acute moral dilemma between his moralism and his adherence to *laissez-faire* was avoided because economic theory had become less 'dismal'. He accepted Say's law that capitalism was a self-equilibriating system because supply created its own demand. He also came to reject the idea that wages were an inexorable and fixed part of the national product. Distribution could be subject to human wishes. Thus, he was far less prepared to endorse the argument that the economy ran according to natural laws, with unpleasant consequences for the working classes. Nevertheless, he was not an advocate of economic growth. For aesthetic and environmental reasons, he wanted a 'stationary state', requiring population control, so that the benefits of increased productivity would improve the income and the leisure time of the individual. As we shall see, Hobson in many respects echoes this perspective.

Mill, in addition, favoured the state regulation of monopolies in communications, gas and water, and land.[31] And in order to bring about a genuine equality of opportunity, a traditional liberal watchword, he advocated greater state interference with the rights of inheritance and bequest.

Mill marked himself off from his utilitarian forebears not only by amending *laissez-faire* principles in specific situations. His approach to the question of the suitability of political institutions was far less naturalistic and more historical and sociological. He saw different forms of political arrangements as appropriate to different societies and historical periods. Thus, anticipating Hobson's own attitude towards the 'lower races', he asserted that 'Despotism is a legitimate mode of government in dealing with barbarians, provided the end be their improvement, and the means justified by actually effecting that end.'[32] He could, moreover, accept with equanimity the idea that socialism in the form of a society based upon co-operatives was a historical possibility.

Finally, his approach to the question of democracy differed from the earlier utilitarians, such as his father, James Mill. He justified it not merely as a protective device against arbitrary rule. It developed the moral and intellectual capacities of citizens.[33] He saw decentralised local government as crucial in fostering this process by enabling greater individual participation in contrast to more centralised types of democracy.[34] As we shall see, Hobson also articulated a similar but not identical position . He paralleled Mill in another way. Mill did not have an unbounded faith in the 'common man'. However much he wanted to include him in democratic decision-making, the educated elite had a key role, especially in initating legislation.[35]

T. H. Green

Influenced by German philosophers, especially Kant and Hegel, Green rejected, as had J. S. Mill, the highly mechanistic and egoistic Benthamite conception of human nature. Human beings were intrinsically social and moral. Individuals derived real, or 'permanent', pleasure not through the satisfaction of appetites, to which they had indeed become enslaved, but through acting upon moral principle for the benefit of the the common good. Society should not, therefore, be seen as consisting of atomised and egoistic individuals, but as a community in which citizen's potentials, especially moral ones, should be realised. The state's function was to create the *conditions* which enabled people to make the 'best' of themselves, which entailed contributing to the common good.[36] It meant, for example, that the freedom of contract, so cherished by the Manchester School, could be subject to state regulation, if such freedom impeded an individual's contribution to the common good, namely in areas such as health and safety at work, unrestricted land ownership and the selling of alcohol. And, for Green, state education played an important role in promoting citizenship. Although his specific proposals were well within the liberal mainstream at the time, he, along with Arnold Toynbee, recognised that a 'crisis' of liberalism was occurring as a result of the emerging disjunction between *laissez-faire* theory and interventionist practice.[37] His teachings had a paradoxical effect on subsequent liberals. Some trod the path of privately organised middle-class philanthropy, taking their cue from his stress on individual self-sacrifice to the community, especially in promoting the moral capacities of the less privileged. Others emphasised his idea that the state was indirectly responsible for the moral welfare of individuals by ensuring that material preconditions existed, necessary for moral action. In both cases, however, liberal reformers were presented with a moral imperative: the creation of circumstances in which the less priviliged members of society could flourish as intrinsically moral beings.

Green's final contribution to the reshaping of the liberal tradition was to historicise liberalism, just as Mill had begun to do. He saw utilitarianism as historically progressive in freeing people from an intellectual tradition that defended privilege, although it had become increasingly intellectually and politically outmoded in terms of its understanding of human nature and its notion of human welfare.

Herbert Spencer

Although it is difficult to gauge accurately the influence of Mill and Green on Hobson, if only because he was notoriously coy about acknowledging his intellectual debts, these two thinkers created an intellectual climate into which he entered. Yet he was candid about the importance of Herbert Spencer in shaping his thought. He did not, though, share Spencer's highly individualistic ideals. His brand of 'survival of the fittest' evolutionism resulted in the call for a hyper-minimal state, dispensing with such functions as the maintenance of lighthouses. Nevertheless, he was responsible for bringing liberalism within the framework of biological explanation, moving it away from Newtonian mechanics, an explanatory paradigm which had found much favour with the utilitarians. In an increasingly godless age, this enabled Hobson to put ethics upon a naturalistic, or 'organic', foundation. Indeed, if there is one all-pervasive metaphor and mode of explanation in Hobson's writings, it is 'organicism'. Hobson saw individuals and society as evolving, interdependent, psycho-biological organisms, and believed that ethics would, and should, develop in such a way that took account of this process. And, in common with Spencer, he believed that competition was vital to progress, although he sharply differed in maintaining that the *form* of competition itself evolved. It was moving away from clashes over physical survival, towards the intellectual and cultural domains. Finally, he was inspired by Spencer's synthetic philosophy that combined history, politics and ethics, as well as biology. Hobson looked at social reality from within a holistic, interdisciplinary framework.[38] He recognised neither the sovereignty nor the autonomy of any particular discipline within the social sciences.

Although there were more immediate influences on Hobson's reworking of classical liberalism – especially Ruskin, William Clarke and various American intellectuals – these three figures were largely responsible for changing the terms of the liberal argument. In effect, they collectively historicised, moralised and 'biologised' liberalism. Following these thinkers, Hobson eschewed the utilitarian's mechanistic, hedonistic and individualistic account of human nature, which saw society as atomised and the state as artificial. He replaced this with a conception that stressed, on the one hand, the psycho-biological roots of human needs and behaviour, and, on the other, a growing capacity for ethical conduct, the genuine sociability of human beings and their ability to get as much satisfaction from 'doing' as consuming. And he employed the organic metaphor (in a way which was quite at odds with Spencer's use of it) in order to demonstrate that the state was no longer 'artificial'. It was the 'brain' of society.[39]

Conclusion

Methodologically, Hobson adopted a far more evolutionary and historical approach than his utilitarian forerunners in his appreciation of the validity and viability of ideas and institutions. It allowed him to cut loose from traditional liberal dogmas, and argue that new ideas and circumstances inevitably pointed to the need to remodel liberal principles. Classical liberalism, whilst progressive in its time, had run its historic course and urgently required updating. This was particularly so on the question of the state and its relation to individual freedom. Negative freedom, which derived from the principle of non-interference, whilst crucial in protecting the individual against arbitrary, aristocratic government, was useless unless citizens had the capacity to act. *Laissez-faire* did not guarantee this capacity on a universal scale. Thus, there was nothing sacrosanct about a minimalist state. The changing functions of the state could be justified as a natural, 'organic' outgrowth of historical forces.

What follows in the subsequent chapters is a closer examination of his endeavour to grapple with the political and ideological crisis of late nineteenth-century liberalism. His attempted resolution worked on four interconnected levels. First, he felt that he had to put his proposed reforms upon a sound philosophical and scientific footing. This necessitated an analysis of human nature, the state and society. It involved the employment of what he considered to be sound scientific methodological principles. Second, a reformulation of liberal political economy was required. This entailed not only methodological and substantive theoretical modifications, and giving due weight to new trends in modern capitalism, especially the growth of monopoly, but also the 'humanisation' of the whole framework of economic thinking. Following Ruskin, Hobson passionately argued that economic thought had to be grounded upon a humanistic ethic which fully took into account the totality of human needs, and which in part transcended the acquisitive and appetitive assumptions of the utilitarians. Thirdly, he saw the realisation of his social reform programme as dependent upon the reform of international relations, especially imperialism, because it diverted political energies and economic resources from the 'Social Problem'. Lastly, there was the practical level: as an intellectual *engagé*, he saw his own political activity as helping to remedy the crisis of liberalism, although it was never his top priority. He became involved in particular campaigns, advocated specific policies and developed, and participated in, political strategies designed to bring his whole project to fruition.

2 The organic perspective

For all Hobson's radicalism — his broadsides against economic orthodoxy and his passionate denunciations of the monopolistic plutocracy and its hangers-on in Parliament, the press, university and church — his aims were, in the real meaning of the term, moderate. He sought to give liberalism a new political and ideological centre of gravity, a new middle ground, that avoided the minimal statism of *laissez-faire* liberalism and what he regarded as the maximal statism of socialism.[1] Through his recentring of liberal theory he hoped to foster a sense of citizenship and community, where social harmony would prevail, and communal and individual 'self-realisation' would flourish. Integral to this project was the promotion of an alliance between middle-class progressives, such as himself, and the working class, inside the Liberal Party or outside it, either in the form of a new political grouping or, as it turned out, inside the Labour Party.

To achieve a durable alliance he believed that his formula for broadening the functions of the state had to be practical without being opportunistic, if only to dispel growing working-class distrust of Liberals.[2] Secondly, such a formula had to protect and promote individual freedom, so dear to Liberals, without sacrificing the principles of social and economic justice. And thirdly, it had to avoid capitulating to monopoly capitalists, or conjuring up a monolithic state machine, the consequence, he believed, of an all-embracing socialism.

In laying the theoretical foundations of his reform programme, he attempted either to synthesise, or to steer between, numerous conflicting values and concepts. The various dichotomies he wanted to reconcile existed, on the one hand, within the liberal tradition – between the hedonism of the utilitarians and the moralism of T. H. Green – and, on the other, between liberal individualism and what he saw as socialist collectivism, which entailed primarily the question of individual/state relations within the economic realm. In broad philosophic terms, his objective was the establishment of a middle position between materialism and idealism, and various cognate antinomies, such as voluntarism and determinism, theory and practice. Additionally, he sought to transcend other 'contradictions', namely, between utopianism and opportunism, and between reason and instinct, facts and values, quantity and quality, science and art. Within economic theory he tried to resolve the traditional antithesis between cost and utility, production and consumption. Finally, as a good pupil of Spencer, he wished to synthesise the various disciplines within the human sciences into a 'sociology', at a time when he felt that they were becoming increasingly specialised, and divorced from each other as well as the real world.

The philosophical and methodological principles that underpinned his reformulated liberalism were expounded and developed in a trio of works, published at roughly fifteen-year intervals: *The Social Problem* (1901), *Work and Wealth* (1914) and *Wealth and Life* (1929). The last two were 'the two big books into which he put most of himself'.[3] Some of his key ideas can be seen in embryonic form in *The Evolution of Modern Capitalism* (1894), particularly the last chapter.[4] These writings display a great consistency of position and attitude, a deepening, rather than a redirection of, focus. In terms of theoretical innovation within Hobson's own intellectual development, *Work and Wealth* contained the greatest. He brought the insights from psychology within the compass of his evolutionary theory. *Wealth and Life* added little to what he had said previously, although it was a far more closely argued, comprehensive and well-structured presentation, in comparison to the other two works. It was effectively a summing up of his life's intellectual endeavour.

The organic perspective

Hobson, like most major social philosophers of his time, was caught up in the backwash of the Darwinian revolution. Whether Marxist, liberal, socialist or conservative, they all turned to the concepts of evolutionary biology for explanation and justification. Hobson developed his own brand of organic evolutionism to gather together multiple dichotomies already referred to. An indication of the hopes that he invested in his organic perspective is evidenced by the following statement: 'The contradiction of production and consumption, cost and utility, physical and spiritual welfare all find their likeliest mode of reconcilement in the treatment of society as an organism.'[5] And in terms of political prescription, organicism was the answer to the crisis of liberalism:

> The real crisis of Liberalism lies ...in the intellectual ability and moral ability to accept and execute a progressive policy which involves a new conception of the functions of the state....in the substitution of an *organic* for an opportunist policy, the adoption of a vigorous definite, positive policy of social reconstruction, involving important modifications in the legal and economic institutions of private property and private industry.[6]

Indeed, his organic perspective constituted the theoretical foundation to his solution to the 'crisis' of late nineteenth-century liberalism.

As a *substantive* theory this perspective contained a vision of individuals and society as evolving organisms. The human being was a part of nature, and could be characterised as a 'psycho-physical organism', or by 'spiritual-animalism'.[7] Humans, though, differentiated themselves from the rest of nature through their mental capacities, which enabled them to become, through evolution, nature's highest product. These qualities developed as a result of their efforts to control and adapt to their environment in order to satisfy their instinctive needs: 'The conception of mankind as working out the human career by the operation of its original supply of faculties and feelings, in which instinctive motives take an increasing admixture of conscious rational guidance, is the key to an understanding of the ascent of man.'[8] Crucially, the growth of reason enabled humans to economise in their energies devoted to basic survival. This economy manifested itself in the growing division of labour and the differentiation of productive function amongst groups and individuals. The human species was developing 'in the sense of gaining more complexity in structure and function for the task of dealing with their environment.'[9] As a result of economy in energy, a 'surplus' was created, over and above that required for physical survival, so establishing the basis for increasing human 'individuation'. With the development of reason, 'The economy of human progress presents a new character, viz., the progressive conquest and adaptation of environment by arts capable of transmission and enabling men to utilise the growing surplus of energy and opportunity over and above the requirements of racial survival.' As a result of the growth of civilisation, human activities became more complex and the individual became more aware of exercising them. And, increasingly, s/he came to have a mind of his or her own, with 'interests and satisfactions which are ingredients of what we call "personality"'.[10] The emergence of 'personality' or 'individuation', expressed in the development of moral, intellectual and aesthetic capacities, signalled the transition from 'quantity' to 'quality' in the evolutionary scale. As the quantitative, 'routine' needs of survival could be more easily met, the surplus of 'organic' energy could be increasingly devoted to 'qualitative' improvement.[11]

Hobson did not, however, equate individuation with the self-regarding individualism of his utilitarian predecessors. Rather, it was accompanied by a growing socialisation of the individual, through necessity and choice. The ever-widening bonds of human interdependence meant that, 'Even the most selfish man in the modern community is compelled constantly to consider the feelings and views of others outside his immediate circle.'[12] Moreover, as the human mind evolved, people would wish to become involved in more co-operative activities: 'As we rise to purely intellectual and moral enjoyments, competition gives way to a generous rivalry in co-operation. In the pursuit of knowledge or goodness, the rivalry is no longer antagonism – what one gains another does not lose. One man's success is not another's failure.'[13] Thus, for Hobson, human evolution, as expressed in the growth of reason and the 'organic' surplus, was characterised by the simultaneous processes of developing individual and social complexity, on the one hand, and the increasing capacity for 'individuation' and social awareness and co-operation, on the other.

Not only did organicism inspire Hobson to construct a substantive evolutionary theory. Equally crucial, it encouraged him to develop a holistic methodological approach in the understanding of individual and societal needs and activities. The need 'to see life steadily and to see it whole' is one of the recurring phrases in his wrtitings.[14] He applauded, rather over-optimistically as it turned out, the 'new tendency to assimilate all "wholes" or unitary systems, from the atom to the universe, mental as well as physical wholes, to the structure and behaviour of an "organism", and see them as systems of interacting parts with internal interrelations on the one hand, and external interrelations with other similarly constructed wholes, on the other...'[15] This methodology was significant for a number of reasons. In the first place, it helped him in coping with what he saw as a fragmented and fragmenting social, political and intellectual universe. It led him to stress the interdependence or interrelatedness of different phenomena. For example, at the level of the individual, Hobson emphasised the interconnection between the activities of production and consumption. Moreover, viewing the world as an interconnected whole provided him with a powerful critique of what he saw as excessive academic specialisation. His holism also led him to think in terms of creating a broad, systematic framework that could unite single-issue social reformers within the Liberal Party in the 1890s. Just as important, at the political level, the notion of human interdependence, which in part stemmed from his holism, induced him to reject the traditional liberal atomistic view of society. For instance, he argued that because wealth was a collective product, the 'collectivity', i.e. the state, ought to have certain powers to decide how that wealth should be distributed. He used his holistic position to attack liberal individualism in another way. For him, society was 'organic' in the sense that it had an identity and 'needs' that were neither reducible to, nor explicable in terms of, the behaviour of its individual 'cells'. Nevertheless, his organic approach allowed him to uphold certain types of liberal individualism, albeit in a modified fashion.

What follows in the rest of this chapter is a closer consideration of, first, how he used his organic perspective – in its substantive and methodological forms – to undermine traditional liberal *laissez-faire* arguments in support of a minimal state, whilst simultaneously avoiding the full embrace of state socialism; and, secondly, how he employed it to establish the theoretical foundations of a practice for social reform. In the next chapter we shall see how it assisted him in supplying an underlying rationale for social and economic reconstruction.

Overcoming the minimal state

He imaginatively and consistently utilised his organic perspective to wean, simultaneously, liberals from their attachment to *laissez-faire*, and socialists from an all-pervasive state. Although he sought to persuade both tendencies to make limited incursions across each other's ideological frontiers, especially before the First World War, he devoted more attention to making liberals feel at home in socialist territory. His organicism created the intellectual framework from which to challenge the fundamental terms of the minimal state argument. As we have already noted in the previous chapter, this argument rested upon an egoistic, hedonistic and acquisitive conception of human nature, and suggested that the state should be solely concerned with 'holding the ring' to ensure that free and fair competition occurred amongst all society's producers and consumers.[16] Thus, the state should devote itself only to the protection of life, property and liberty (defined in the 'negative' sense of non-interference from others). This set the boundaries of the state's commitment in looking after the welfare of its citizens.

Hobson, in seeking to widen the economic and social functions of the state, had to weaken the force of the argument against active, paternalist government, and establish that, at least in principle, the state could possess the knowledge and capacity to look after certain elements of individual welfare better than the individual. Indeed, he defined welfare in such a way that it transcended the hedonistic utilitarian definition, based on individual wants, so as to include 'needs'. In fact, his organic perspective drove him well beyond the terrain of utilitarian individualism to suggest that society itself had legitimate 'needs', that a collective, 'general will', which could be separate from an individual's immediate desires, should rightfully exist. Hence, he had to persuade liberals that it could be proper for a representative state to be in some sense the custodian of this 'general will'.

Defining welfare

In defining the nature of human welfare, Hobson used his organicism to unite and transcend utilitarian hedonism and T. H. Green's moralism, with its religious overtones. He viewed hedonism in historical terms. It was a necessary phase in human evolution towards greater individuation, a form of selfishness that was an expression of the emergence of human reason. It signified that individuals could have goals separate from the instinctive community. The growing abundance of physical resources facilitated this individuation:

> The increasing supply of foods and other sources of physical satisfaction [the individual] may apply to build up for himself a life of super-brutal hedonism. For when reason first begins to assert supremacy, it is apt to become thrall to the purely animal self.[17]

Yet, utilitarianism's hedonistic assumption meant that it could have no universal application. It was incapable of distinguishing between the actually desired and the desirable[18] and its hedonistic calculus rendered it useless in the consideration of social costs and benefits.[19]

Furthermore, his evolutionary perspective convinced him that human beings possessed a potential that took them beyond the fixation with immediate physical satisfaction. Nevertheless, there was an earthiness and earthliness about Hobson that led him to reject the abstract and quasi-religious moralism of T. H. Green. This opposition may have had something to do with his rejection in the mid-1890s of the individualistic philosophy of the London Ethical Society, which was run by two of T. H. Green's followers, Bernard Bosanquet and J. H. Muirhead, and his transfer of membership to the more collectivist South Place Ethical Society.[20] Indeed, he felt closer to the utilitarians. He identified welfare and its values 'with conscious satisfactions, so rescuing Ethics from vague conceptions of self-realisation, in order to make it a New Utilitarianisn, in which physical and moral satisfactions will rank in their places'.[21] He constantly stressed that he was seeking to formulate a 'New Utilitarianism'.[22]

He explicitly avoided the privileging of ethical conduct as the highest value. This was an example of what he called the 'monadist, or separatist fallacy – the refusal to see life as an organic whole'.[23] 'The "good life" embodied the "truly desirable" in every shape and form.'[24] Language itself demonstrated that ethics had no special status. The term 'right' had an aesthetic origin, and this accounted for the fact that '"straight" and "crooked" conduct have a stronger purchase on most minds than "good" or "bad".'[25] Moreover, ordinary speech demonstrated the difficulty in separating moral values from intellectual or aesthetic ones, or the latter values from the former. 'Good' was not merely a moral term. It could be applied to health, luck, a hypothesis or portrait. 'True' was not only an intellectual or philosophical value: it could refer to an eye, measure or a friend. 'Beautiful' was not just an aesthetic term: it could refer to character, a solution to a problem or a surgical operation.[26]

Hobson was reluctant to claim that any of these 'higher' values were worth more in themselves. 'This is the snare of the intellectualist, as pedant, or "high-brow", of the moralist, as prig or Pharisee.'[27] Individuals entered society 'body and soul' and carried into it 'the inseparable character of the organic life, with all the physical and spiritual activities and purposes it contains'.[28] Indeed, values, he insisted, 'were not found in the higher abstractions of philosophical thought, but in the lower levels of human nature – the instincts, appetites and behaviour of animal man'.[29] Nevertheless, he conceded that a distinction could be made between 'higher' and 'lower' values in the sense that the former were higher because they were an expression of a higher stage of human evolution, associated with increasing 'individuation'.[30] As individuality and a personal life came to play a more significant part 'in the economy of evolution, activities and satisfactions closely related to the mind will figure more prominently as values or sources of value'.[31] Happiness would be raised to a higher level. Yet these values could not realised at the expense of satisfying 'lower' needs, for the former were dependent upon the latter. Human progress required 'that one after another the lower material animal functions shall be reduced to routine in order that a larger amount of individual effort may be devoted to the exercise of higher functions...'.[32] Thus, he hoped that evolution would eventually unite the desired with the desirable.

Human nature, community and state

Hobson deployed his organic perspective not only to determine the meaning of human welfare. It aided him in demonstrating the existence of, and possibility of realising, a general will. First, he insisted that society was an 'organism'. It had a distinct identity and needs in some sense separate from its members. His organic view led him to reject different forms of theoretical individualism that justified the minimal state or denied the existence of a general will. He opposed the ontological individualist position that 'society does not exist, only individuals'. Rather, he maintained that society exists precisely in 'the co-operation of individuals'.[33] He departed from the methodological individualism of those, such as his friend Hobhouse, who explained the existence and character of society in terms of individual dispositions.[34] Different forms of collective life could not be reduced to the 'ideas, feelings and actions of individual persons', or be explained as the outcome of 'social contracts of free individuals seeking by co-operation to forward their own individual ends'.[35] 'On this basis', he said, 'the acts of devotion and self-sacrifice, and still more the acts of preparatory skill, the elaborate performance of deeds that are means to the survival and well-being of a future generation, become mere haphazard miracles.'[36] This individualist explanation of society was how it looked *'from the standpoint of the cell'*.[37] Yet in reality humanity in all its various aggregations was ' a social stuff, and ... whatever forms of coalescence it assumes, i.e. a nation, caste, church, party, etc., there will exist a genuine organic unity, a central or general life, strong or weak' which was 'distinct and dominant over the life of its members'.[38] Although he was not fully satisfied with the term 'organism', he thought it helped people realise ' that all life proceeds by the co-operation of units working, not each for its own separate self, but for a whole, and attaining their separate well-being in the proper functioning of that whole'.[39]

Hobson also used an 'organic' explanation to demonstrate that the associative mode of individual behaviour, the necessary condition for a general will, was rooted in human instinct, which was required for the self-protection and advancement of their species. Individual altruistic action could be understood in terms of the 'higher' rationality of species survival and growth, of which the individual may be unaware.[40] This other-regarding instinct, he believed, had not disappeared in the modern world, although the more obvious bonds of community had been lost through growing individual and group differentiation. This was because instinctive altruism had become 'rationalised', albeit imperfectly, allowing individual loyalty to transcend that of the immediate group (family, tribe, etc.) and to extend to wider (Hobson hoped, world) collectivities. 'The advancing reason in the individual animal may consist in a growing sympathy and syn-noesis with the wider organism.'[41] Industrialisation was central to the development of this sympathy that was beginning to assume global proportions. It was, he asserted, the most powerful instrument of education. It had done more 'to rationalise and socialise men than all the higher and more spiritual institutions of man, so far as such comparisons are possible'.[42]

Not only did he utilise his organic conception to show how the general will, in the first instance, was embedded in human nature. It served as a theoretical device to counter the liberal objection to a state becoming paternalistic through increasing its welfare functions. Such a process, for Hobson, was a further indication of the rationalisation of human survival and growth instincts, a desire to create a surplus of 'organic' energy above that required to meet survival needs. The state was a 'rational' and 'natural' outcome of this evolutionary process, necessary to generate this surplus energy. The instincts for growth and survival were 'accompanied by corresponding emotions, which, according to the degree of intelligence they contain, impel it to a right or economical use of the physical and spiritual environment for survival and "progress"'. The instinctive and emotional 'stream of the common life' became 'more "rational" as the factors of intelligence accompanying the emotions become clearer, better co-ordinated and endowed with a larger capacity for central direction'. There emerged 'a flexible general instinct operating through a centralised nervous system and co-ordinating the special organic emotions and activities to serve a more clearly conceived organic purpose of the individual or the race'.[43]

Thus, government was central in realising this 'organic purpose' (which can be broadly described as individual and communal self-realisation), and it was strictly analogous to a brain. It was the 'sensorium' of society. Hence, Hobson could justify the existence of a paternalistic, 'expert governing class'. 'The cerebral centres, the expert governing class' determined 'the organic policy', but they did so on the basis of the mass of information transmitted from the 'cells'. The detailed execution of policy was directed by the 'cells', which distributed 'the work in accordance with adjustments of cellular self-interest that are not referred to the central power.'[44]

Given the importance of experts within his organic theory, not surprisingly he rejected the political individualism contained in the slogan 'one man, one vote', one of the premises of the anti-paternalistic argument. It implied that one man's contribution to government was as good as any other's.[45] Nevertheless, consistent with his desire to effect a compromise between individualism and collectivism, he maintained that the jurisdiction of experts be confined to physical needs, and not to those of a 'higher' nature, which should be left to the individual.[46]

Interfering with property

In suggesting that the state, as a 'sensorium', could embody the 'general will and wisdom' of society, Hobson set the scene for his justification of the state's abridgement of private property rights. Compared to the individual, it could have superior knowledge in the administration of society's resources. Other aspects of his organicism helped legitimate state interference in this sphere. First, the growth of human individuation was contingent upon the socialisation of the lower routine functions, associated with the satisfaction of material survival needs. The socialisation of these functions, i.e. the state control of industries that met survival needs, enhanced the amount of 'organic energy' required for the cultivation of higher qualities through the 'stoppage of lower forms of competition'.[47] Significantly, this argument enabled Hobson to undercut the Social Darwinist defence of *laissez-faire*. The socialisation of the lower functions allowed the plane of competition to evolve: 'a larger amount of individual effort may be devoted to the exercise of higher functions and the cultivation by strife of higher qualities'.[48] This competition was essentially non-antagonistic: 'In the pursuit of knowledge or goodness the rivalry is no longer antagonism – what one gains another does not lose. One man's success is not another's failure.'[49]

Secondly, his organic vision enabled him to attack the argument that individual property rights were absolute. He dismissed the notion that business was purely private or self-regarding in character, because of the 'complex social nature of every commercial act. So soon as the idea of a social industrial organism is grasped, the question of state interference in, or state assumption of, an industry becomes a question of social expediency – that is, of the just interpretation of the facts relating to a particular case.'[50] In Hobson's eyes such 'facts' had to do primarily with whether that industry satisfied routine needs through machine production and had become monopolistic.

Indeed, because he saw society as 'a maker of values', rather than the individual, he could justify the state, as representative of society, in redistributing income. He gave the example of a shoemaker to demonstrate the social character of production.

> The value of a pair of shoes which he 'produces', by working by himself, is as much determined by society as the land-values of [a] farmer, as soon as they begin to emerge. The skill and knowledge of his craft is an elaborate social product, and is taught him by society; the same society protects him while he works, assists him by an elaborate organisation of markets to get leather, tools, thread, and a work-place, provides him with a market in the form of persons who have evolved the need of wearing boots, and the industrial arts whereby to pay for them, and so forth. The value of the boots when made will obviously depend, to an indefinite extent, upon the innumerable factors which affect the supply and demand of all other products, along with which boots figure in processes of exchange.[51]

In embellishing his argument that the state had a claim on the wealth created by individuals, he maintained that the existence of co-operation itself enabled them to produce a quantity of output that was greater than the mere sum of their separate inputs.[52] This helped to create a 'social surplus' above that required to sustain the individual in production, to which the state was entitled. Indeed, the state's expenditure on health, education, etc. meant that it, too, was a factor of production, contributing to economic output, and required, therefore, an income in the form of taxation to sustain this role.[53]

His final argument in favour of the abridging of private property rights entailed turning the Hegelian-based defence of property used by Bosanquet and others on its head. His 'ontological holism', namely, that the community could have interests distinct from its members, led him to claim that the state itself required property for the community's self-realisation, in the form of collective goods such as education, sanitation, public buildings, etc.[54]

Yet Hobson's objective, in accord with his desire to unite individualism and collectivism, did not imply the total elimination of individual political and property rights. Individual political rights, he asserted, should be conserved within a system of government, conceived as federal in form. There existed 'an area of individual liberty' that was 'conducive to the heart of the collective life'.[55] 'It can never be in the interests of society to attempt to dominate or enslave the individual, sucking his energies for the supposed nutriment of the state.'[56] Without such individual contributions, that state could not be maintained or develop in its functions. Thus, 'Each limb, each cell, has a "right" to its supply of blood.'[57] These 'rights' included those of 'suggestion, protest, veto, and revolt'.[58] In terms of individual/state relations, he substituted the minimalist symmetry of the passive citizen/passive state, for the active citizen/active state. The active, paternalistic state had to be counterbalanced by active, socially conscious individuals. This required the further democratisation of the state. For example, before the First World War, he called not only for the abolition of the House of Lords veto but also for the democratisation of the House of Commons: 'By securing an extended franchise [most probably to cover women], shorter parliaments and adequate reforms of electoral machinery, representives might at least become a genuine expression of the popular will.'[59] In addition, he wanted to bring the civil service closer to society by promoting greater equality of opportunity for all sections of the population to enter the profession. At the same time, he wished to draw citizens closer to the state. He wanted 'a growth of public intelligence and conscience as shall establish the real final control of the Government for Society in its full organic structure'.[60] Later, he saw industrial democracy as a crucial instrument in creating an ethos of active citizenship.[61]

As for property rights, he aimed to effect an equitable reconciliation between state and individual claims upon the social product. Both the individual and society needed property to survive and develop: 'Let the individual and society each own, out of the property they jointly create, that portion which is necessary to support the life and sustain the progress of each.'[62] Specifically, this reconciliation entailed the complete abolition of all unearned income, 'so that all property is clearly earned either by individuals or by societies'.[63] Only then could an ethical basis be laid for an industrial society: 'When all property is visibly justified alike in its origin and use, the rights of property will for the first time be respected, for they will for the first time be respectable.'[64]

Although keen to preserve individual political and property rights, he maintained that in reality the antithesis between the individual and society was a false one, as 'unthinkable as the notion of a conflict of interests between the trunk of a tree and its branches'.[65] It was the result of misconceiving the individual as a '*mere* isolated unit'.[66]

> Only so long as we confine our attention to the body is the illusion of absolute individuality plausible; directly we realise the individual as a 'person', a rational being, a spirit or soul, we perceive he lives and moves and has his being in society, and that his 'ends' as an individual are organically related to and determined by the social ends.[67]

Moreover, Hobson held that society itself was the creator of individual freedom. Through providing the framework for material and spiritual co-operation, it enabled individuals continually 'to enlarge the quantity and to raise the quality of their interests, aims and satisfactions'.[68]

Laying the theoretical foundations of practice

Hobson's evolutionary schema helped him to unite the theory and practice of social reform. In asserting that human evolution was an expression of, and was fostered by, the growth of human reason, not surprisingly he saw theory as essential to the practice of social reform: 'The supreme condition of social progress is for a society to "know itself".'[69] This would enable the 'conscious, rational ordering of [society's] resources' through the elimination of waste, or what he later described as the 'unproductive surplus'.[70] In this process, science had a crucial role. It directed the 'silent, instinctive organic strivings of mankind' in order to help achieve their ends in a more economical fashion. It 'enlightened common-sense'. An 'economy' of 'blind instincts' in a 'rapidly changing and complex environment' would be subject to 'enormous vital wastes'. What was needed was a 'general instinct of adaptability of means to ends, involving conscious reflection'. Reason, he urged was 'this general instinct and science its instrument'.[71]

However, for Hobson science had to be subordinated to the *art* of social progress, which was essentially about qualitative improvement. Science could not measure differences of kind, and thus could not provide a criterion for evaluating economic or social policy, just as it could not tell the difference between good and bad works of art. For example: 'Financial policy is an artistic or creative work in which quantities are used, but do not direct or dominate.'[72] Science was incapable of coping with the uniqueness of a phenomenon: 'the uniqueness of the individual organism and the novelty of each of its changes are an assertion of the qualitative nature of the subject matter'.[73] Nevertheless, science could be employed where 'human nature is uniform and stable among the units which constitute the life whose conduct and welfare are in question'.[74] Hence, it could be applied where production and consumption were uniform and routine. For instance, in the distribution of life's necessities, it could demonstrate first, that an equal distribution of a product would tend to produce a larger aggregate utility or satisfaction in consumption compared with an unequal distribution of the product, and, secondly, that if a measurement of relative needs of consumers were possible, an unequal distribution, proportionate to needs, would yield a still larger aggregate amount of satisfaction.[75]

One crucial implication of his desire to speed up human progress through getting society to 'know itself' was the need for a unified approach to the human or social sciences. Taking his cue from Spencer and Comte, he insisted that the various disciplines concerned with human facts, ranging from physiology and psychology to economics, ethics and politics, had to be brought within a 'federation' of subjects, collectively entitled 'sociology'. These studies, in order to be useful to reformers required co-ordination: '... the broader human setting, demanded for the judgement or the policy of a statesman or reformer, can never be obtained by [a] separatist treatment. For the interactions which relate these [social] issues to one another are numerous and intimate.'[76] For example, in considering working-class welfare, questions of wages, hours and regularity of employment overlapped, as did those of housing, food, drink, education, recreation and transport.

In practical political terms, such a holistic methodology was imperative as a result of the fragmentation and excessive specialisation of social reformers: '...the practical reformer had narrowed the phrase ['The Social Question'] to connote Drink, Sex Relations, Population, or even Money...'.[77] What was required was 'a fuller consciousness among those different fields of thought and work...a recognition of their unity of purpose and a fruitful co-operation'.[78] This would enable social reformers to avoid squandering their energies. Hobson also claimed that over-specialisation was a manifestation of a paralysis of the reforming impulse within the academic community.[79] The demands of fame and gain, or disinterested concerns with immediate problems, or sheer intellectual conservativism caused this over-specialisation. Consequently, the academic seldom reached any definite opinion upon 'living issues'. He could seldom find such an opinion justified.

'His abandonment of the wider survey of knowledge...destroys intellectual judgement. Every bit of new knowledge needs to be assayed by submission to the touchstone of the Universal before its value can be ascertained, or it can be set in relation to knowledge as a whole.' Man was the measure of all things, and the 'specialist who has made himself less than a man can measure nothing. The industrial specialist becomes a machine, the intellectual specialist a pedant or a faddist.'[80]

Not only did over-specialisation undermine the impulse to reform, the ethical imperative also became lost through a separation of facts and values, especially as a result of employing the inductive method. On the contrary, Hobson argued that, the 'ought' was not something separate and distinct from the 'is'. Rather, the 'ought' was 'everywhere the highest aspect of, or relation of, an "is".' If a 'fact' had a moral import, it stemmed from being 'part of the nature of the fact, and the fact cannot be fully known as fact without taking it [i.e. the moral import] into consideration'.[81] He countered the inductivist's charge that introducing a standard of utility (i.e. values) was illegitimately importing a priori ethics into the social sciences. The ordering of crude facts in the first instance depended upon the use of a priori principles. Moreover, one could not investigate phenomena effectively 'without possessing some clear motive for investigation, and this motive will be related to a wider motive, which will eventually relate to some large speculative idea', which contained some notion of political or social good.[82]

Since the social sciences were irreducibly ethical and a priori in nature, he concluded that economics was a 'branch of human conduct'. And this *demands a change in the conception of an economic science...involving a recognition that every operative "ought" is an "is" and must be taken into account of in any analysis of economic facts and forces*.[83] Precisely because he wanted to give economics an overt ethical underpinning, he had to integrate it into his holistic social scientific framework. From his 'organic' perspective, a constant interaction occurred between an individual's or a groups's economic and non-economic activities. The former activities had to be seen in terms of their good or bad effects upon the individual or social organism.[84]

Nevertheless, he accepted the autonomy of economics within his 'federation' of 'sociology', in so far as it confined 'itself to the study of industry as a group of objective phenomena...'.[85] Within this context he endorsed Alfred Marshall's definition of economics as 'getting and spending' as analytically separable from other disciplines. But because the 'conscious life' which these 'getting and spending' activities expressed, 'the real subjective import which they bear, does not show them separate or separable, but organically interwoven with other feelings and other intellectual activities'.[86] And thus economics had to be brought within a broader 'organic' or humanistic framework of study, where the subjective, or psychological and physiological, dimensions of these objective activities could be considered.

In sum, the study of economics could be incorporated within his larger 'organic' project that facilitated the self-knowledge of society, and supplied the basis for political and economic practice, thereby quickening human progress. Economics as an autonomous analysis of industry as a 'going concern' could be united with other 'subjective' disciplines – ethics, psychology, physiology, etc – to enable society's and its members' activities to be organised in a less wasteful fashion. Exactly how his economic analysis in its objective and subjective aspects underpinned his proposals for social reform will be the subject of the next chapter.

Conclusion

Hugh Dalton, later to become Chancellor of the Exchequer in the 1945-51 Labour government, in reviewing *Work and Wealth*, was non-plussed by Hobson's organic perpective: 'let it be said that Mr Hobson is somewhat obsessed by the "organic". Such phrases as

"organic welfare", "organic standpoint", "organic value" occur with
a frequency out of all proportion to their significance. For in truth
they mean very little.'[87] What this chapter has sought to demonstrate is just how meaningful the term 'organic' was for Hobson
in trying to remedy the 'crisis' of late nineteenth-century
liberalism'. It enabled him to justify the broadening of the state's
economic and welfare functions, while simultaneously assuaging
Liberal fears of a leviathan state. Collectivist measures did not have
to be regarded as 'exceptions' to *laissez-faire*. Instead, they could
be seen as a 'natural' outcome of human evolution, of a 'general
will' grounded in human instinct, whose goal was individual and
societal survival and development. Thus, he overcame the minimalist
defence through a redefinition of human welfare that straddled the
materialism of the utilitarians and the idealism of T. H. Green, by
the use of the concept of human evolution. The state had a positive
role to play in furthering this process, especially in economising on
the energy required for physical survival.

The state was not only an expression of evolving rationality, of
the collective mastery of human beings over nature and their own
society. In its democratised form, as a function of the general will,
it was a manifestation of the human instinct of solidarity. And
Hobson justified its increased directive role in an 'organic' way, by
suggesting that it was the 'sensorium' of society. Finally, this
perspective assisted him in his argument for curtailing individual
property rights. Wealth was the product of an 'organically' co-
operative society, and the state, as representative of that society,
had the right to use it for the purposes of individual and collective
welfare. Yet, he did not lose sight of traditional liberal values. The
aim of socialising 'routine' industries was to promote
'individuation', which he regarded as vital to human progress.
Equally, he saw increased democratic rights as essential, not only
to combat the forces of reaction but also to ensure that an enlarged
state was accountable. Furthermore, these rights were an ex-

pression of a natural desire to participate in communal life.

His organic perspective had a function apart from justifying increased state intervention in economic life. It was 'progressive' in another sense. It helped generate a movement demanding such intervention. He insisted that it would help society to 'know itself', and promote the more effective deployment of disparate and often uninformed reforming energies. An 'organic', holistic view of the human sciences was vital in bringing various disciplines within the federative structure of 'sociology'. This would encourage social reformers to acknowledge the interconnection of social problems, to assess the full impact of their proposed reforms and to suggest the most efficient method of co-ordinating their efforts.

Finally, at a theoretical level, we have seen how his organic perspective enabled him to give numerous antinomies, such as hedonism/moralism, reason/instinct, facts/values and science/art, a place within an evolutionary system.

3 Political economy

Hobson's evolutionary organic framework enabled him to unite a theory and practice of social reform. Human beings, through gaining greater knowledge of their social and economic environment, exercised increasing mastery over it, in order to achieve greater individual and communal 'self-realisation'. At the centre of his intellectual endeavours was an attempt to articulate an economic theory with overtly practical implications for the functions of the modern state. He sharply criticised orthodox political economy for its espousal of *laissez-faire* and its attendant inability to provide the state with a rationale needed to realise a progressive, humanist ethic. It was utterly inadequate in explaining and diagnosing the 'Social Problem'. Although in many respects he worked within the categories of orthodox economics, he nevertheless developed his own distinctive framework, powerfully shaped by his own organic perspective and by the writings of John Ruskin.

Ruskin

Hobson's moral critique of capitalism and his ethical rationale for economic reform were directly inspired by Ruskin's teachings.[1] He made Ruskin's saying 'there is no wealth but life' into his own personal motto, a motto he was never tired of repeating. From him, Hobson drew the 'basic thought' for his 'subsequent economic writings, viz. the necessity of going behind the current monetary estimates of wealth, cost and utility, to reach the body of human benefits and satisfactions that gave them real meaning'.[2] Hobson strongly maintained that a given body of wealth had to be measured not by money but in terms of the real human costs of creating it, and real human satisfactions that it yielded. The less production entailed creative and spontaneous activity and the more it involved toil and monotony, the greater the human cost, whatever its price. Indeed, Hobson wholeheartedly shared Ruskin's desire to mitigate the disutilities of work by making it as self-expressive as possible, so that ideally the interactions of productive and consumptive activities ought to be 'realised as a fine art'.[3] And as for consumption, the price of a commodity bore no relation to its instrinsic worth. It could be poor in quality or harmful, as in the case of alcohol. Such goods contained 'illth', as opposed to wealth. They also possessed an 'effectual value'. This depended upon the capacity of the consumer to derive benefit from it, and was determined by such factors as whether the consumer was sated, or suffered from ill-health or fatigue derived from overwork. Here Hobson took Ruskin's cue and saw the activities of production and consumption as 'organically' interlinked. Hence, in making a proper 'calculus' of objective wealth, important questions arose as to how work and consumption actually were, and ought to be, distributed amongst the population in terms of an individual's capacity both to produce and consume.

Hobson went some of the way in accepting Ruskin's explanation for these disutilities of production and consumption. Capitalist competition, modern machine production and the growing division of labour were responsible for robbing work of its expressive significance, producing poor-quality goods as well as inequitably distributing them. Moreover, competition generated a hugely wasteful selling process.

Finally, Hobson warmly applauded Ruskin's debunking of the scientific pretensions of orthodox political economy, which he had described as 'the economy of the shrewd Lancashire mill-owner "writ large" and called political'.[4] Ruskin rejected its materialism, its faith in competition and its adherence to a monetary standard of value. Further, he disliked the presentation of economic laws as natural, operating independently of human will. He insisted that political economy could be an 'art', as well as a 'science', thereby legitimating state intervention in the economy for ethical ends.[5]

Beyond the more specific influence of Ruskin's economic insights, Hobson strongly approved of his diatribes against the luxury and idleness of the upper classes. In particular, he rephrased, in his own organic fashion, one of Ruskin's biblical injunctions: 'whosoever will not work, neither *can* he eat.'[6]

Yet, he was by no means Ruskin's blinkered disciple. He disliked his advocacy of a benevolent aristocracy, and his rejection of democracy.[7] He reproached him for understressing the disutilities of labour in production, whilst overstressing those attached to consumption.[8] And Ruskin failed to examine the relationship between different kinds of effort and satisfaction, in order that a 'rational standard of the good life may be established which shall economise most perfectly the powers of the individual'.[9] Lastly, he held that Ruskin's treatment of value was defective. In making it intrinsic and eternal, it became independent of consumer estimates. Hobson's own evolutionary perspective, on the other hand, led him to take a relativist position: value was a function of the cultural stage that a particular society had reached.[10]

Critique of political economy

In order to comprehend why Hobson formulated his own, 'heretical' brand of economics, his rejection of conventional economic wisdom must be understood. Much of his critique of orthodox political economy was informed by Ruskin's teachings and his own organic perspective in its substantive and methodological modes. He also questioned its empirical veracity and subjected it to an internal, ethical critique. It was incapable of realising the very values — economic justice, freedom and equality — that it claimed to promote.

He raised a number of general objections against it, both in its classical and neo-classical variants (the former concentrated on the objective costs of production, the latter on the subjective utilities of consumption). As a true disciple of Ruskin, he disliked its narrowness of focus in effectively making the goal of production paramount, and thereby ruling out wider considerations of human welfare.[11] He disagreed with orthodox political economy's identification of wealth and its monetary evaluation, on the one hand, with human welfare, on the other. It ignored the human costs to, and utilities of, both the producers and the consumers of a given body of wealth. Moreover, it overlooked the two sets of 'organic'interactions between the acts of production and consumption in relation to the individual, and between economic and non-economic life with respect to overall individual welfare.[12]

There were other problems associated with the monetary estimate of wealth. First, it could measure the value of only those goods which were marketed and not those 'free' goods that did not enter into exchange, such as public land.[13] Second, a logical difficulty arose: the qualitative differences between costs and utilities could not be translated into quantitative, monetary terms, a problem that has bedevilled the utilitarian tradition from John Stuart Mill onwards: 'The essential character of every organic subject-matter is that it presents qualitative differences which cannot be reduced to terms of a common denominator.'[14] Pleasures and values of different kinds were incommensurable.

Political economy's attempts at quantification were an expression of the desire to make economics into an exact science. Hobson, however, riduculed its scientific pretensions. As a 'huxter science', it could not be a useful guide in solving the practical problems of unemployment and poverty.[15] He wrote with a scorn that could not have endeared him to the fraternity of academic economists: 'Men of humane culture, smitten with social compunction, and hard-headed self-educated working men, have turned for light and leading to text books of economic science, and have found darkness; have gone for bread, and have received the stones of arid, barren academic judgements.'[16]

He articulated one further general criticism: he rejected the assumption that the market system justly distributed rewards. In *The Economics of Distribution* (1900), he aimed to prove that in most bargaining situations participants were unequally matched. Force or cunning decided the issue. In particular, echoing Adam Smith (*Wealth of Nations*, Book 1, Chapter 8), he noted that capitalists could invariably afford to delay transactions and therefore got the better of workers, who had to work or starve.[17]

Classical economics

His specific objections to classical economics stemmed, first, from the spurious claim of its practitioners that it was a disinterested science. Rather, it served to legitimate the interests of a rising capitalist class, through, among other things, 'the rationalisation of the acquisitive instinct'.[18] Hence, it was obsessed with the production of marketable goods, ignored questions of distribution and considered consumption only in so far as it was either 'productive' or 'non-productive', especially whether it increased the productivity of labour.[19]

He also challenged assumptions that lay behind classical economy's advocacy of a 'simple system of natural liberty' enshrined in the doctrine of *laissez-faire*. It was not 'so "simple" as it sounds'.[20] The welfare of society as a whole could not be achieved through the promotion of economic liberty, which enabled individuals to pursue their own self-interests. Too many questions were begged. It offended his holistic methodology in falsely assuming that the arithmetical aggregation of individual interests was identical to the common interest. And, secondly, it wrongly held that by giving economic freedom to 'each', 'all' would benefit – in the absence of equal access to the factors of production – through the filtering down of wealth to the rest of the community.[21] Finally, to presume that society consisted solely of self-seeking individuals revealed an impoverished conception of human nature. This was in part the product of an ahistorical approach, and led political economists to hold a fixed, mechanical view of society, and a belief that *laissez-faire* was appropriate to all peoples at all times and places.[22]

Neo-classical economics

As for neo-classical economics, although Hobson approved of its starting point in the analysis of consumption, he did not see it as much of a fundamental improvement upon its classical predecessor. Marketable wealth remained, effectively, the dominant consideration.[23] It failed to express 'concrete economic goods and economic processes in terms of human welfare',[24] and it did not have a unified theory of distribution.[25] Indeed, it was in a sense worse than classical economics, since it consisted of a number of separate theories, and was therefore unable to provide a systematic framework for economic analysis.[26]

He found fault with all the leading neo-classical economists of his day. Jevons overlooked the disutilities of production.[27] Marshall, although he reconciled the cost and utility schools of value by showing both as part of the law of supply and demand, did not explore the subjective costs of economic activity.[28] And Pigou not only shared Jevons's weakness in failing to examine the disutilities of production, he illegitimately equated objective wealth with human welfare, and assessed utility solely in terms of current desirability, without considering the intrinsic merits of each commodity.[29]

However, Hobson's real *bête noire* was marginalism, the key tool of neo-classical analysis. It helped to restore 'confidence in the natural equity and efficiency of the economic system as it stands'.[30] He particularly disliked the way in which it ruled out the possibility of an unearned surplus, which, as we shall see, was the centrepiece of his own empirical and normative analysis of capitalism. It supposed that all units received as much value as they produced, i.e. that they were paid what they were worth.[31] For Hobson, this deeply offensive moral conclusion rested upon deeply flawed assumptions, which reflected a general tendency within economics to become a quantitative science, amenable to mathematical analysis. Marginalism's technical deficiencies stemmed from what could be defined as a false reductionism. First, it wrongly attributed 'a separate productivity and a separate value to the marginal increment of a simple or composite factor of production'.[31] The holistic element in his organic perspective prompted him to argue that entrepreneurs did not work out the appropriate combination of inputs on the basis of separate, marginal productivities of each factor of production. Instead, they formulated an overall plan, an 'organic structure', in which all factors interacted.[32] Thus, the Law of Diminishing Returns which marginalists attributed to each factor of production simply meant in reality 'that in any line of industry there are efficient types of business which cannot be increased in size without damage'.[33] At any given time there was room only for a specific number of businesses or plants, which all tended to possess similar levels of productivity and profit. Hobson concluded from this that supply prices were not determined by marginal costs of the different factors of production, but by 'the normal average cost of production for a unit of supply in a representative business'.[34]

Connected with this manifestation of marginalism's false reductionism was the presupposition that the units of supply were infinitely divisible. For Hobson, on the other hand – and here he followed Marshall – the true unit of supply was the representative business or plant. So that if demand rose only slightly there would not tend to be an increase in supply. Rather, there had to be a significant increase in demand, in terms of size and consistency, before it would be matched by an increase in supply, through the addition of representative plants or businesses to the industry.[35] Similarly, on the consumption side, demand was not affected by small 'insensible price changes'.[36] Instead, Hobson maintained that it was 'the standard of living in a representative family, or group that determines how many units of this or that article of consumption shall be demanded'.[37] The consumption of particular goods was determined by an overall plan, which was an 'organic complex'. Changes in consumption tended to occur in a dramatic fashion, as a function of changes in consumption plans, stemming from such things as changes in taste, or the imposition of a heavy tax on commodities.[38]

Finally, Hobson doubted whether money could be used to redefine consumer preferences, in reducing the qualitative to the quantitive. Marginalists assumed that the composition of an individual's consumption was the product of marginal expenditures on each item of consumption yielding similar amounts of satisfaction. But to presume that the consumer compared the marginal values of different kinds of satisfaction was psychologically false. Effects were wrongly ascribed to causes. 'So far as it is true that the last sovereign of my expenditure in bread equals in utility the last sovereign of my expenditure in books, that fact proceeds not from a comparison, conscious or unconscious, of these separate items at this margin, but from the parts assigned respectively to bread and books in the organic plan of my life.'[39] So, for example, if an individual's income changed and marginal adjustments occurred, this was not the result of making marginal comparisons, but of the effect of a change in the overall plan or standard of consumption.

Hobson felt, therefore, that conventional economics in its different varieties was unfit for the task of laying the ground rules for state intervention in the economy, aimed at promoting human welfare. It contained no unified and comprehensive set of explanatory principles. It implicitly or explicitly endorsed an unreformed capitalist system. Its narrow obsession with the production of marketable commodities and with precision and quantification led it illegitimately to identify wealth with welfare. It was unable to explain the actual behaviour of both producers and consumers, or to demonstrate that *laissez-faire* capitalism advanced economic freedom and justice or that it created a genuine equality of economic opportunity, for the mass of the population.

Hobson, in wishing to reform capitalism, constructed his own alternative version of political economy, which did not, he hoped, suffer from the same theoretical deficiencies. He had to address a number of key questions. What precisely was wrong with capitalism, both in terms of ethics and efficiency, i.e. how should capitalism's malady be diagnosed? Secondly, how was the malady to be explained? Thirdly, what remedies were required to overcome these ills? The last question will be considered in the next chapter.

Diagnosing the malady: the 'New Utilitarianism'

The organic criterion

In order to assess adequately the ills of capitalism, its inability to meet human needs, he established an external reference point, a standard of 'organic' human welfare, to show what needs were not being met.

He was the first to admit that his own criterion did not possess the exactitude of orthodox political economy. It involved qualitative, as well as quantitative, considerations, for instance, when looking at the multiple impact of economic processes on non-economic activities, such as home life, intellectual, political and social pursuits.[40] Moreover, there were differences of individual personality, and environments in which individuals were situated, so that every person derived dissimilar satisfactions, making an arithmetical aggregation of pleasures difficult.[41] This problem was compounded because the 'arts' of production and consumption were continually changing, and so therefore were human costs and utilities attached to a given income.[42] Almost as if deliberately to upset the mathematical proclivities of modern economists, he offered his own 'true criterion' of economic welfare. It was rooted in the 'silent, instinctive organic strivings of mankind'.[43] And it consisted of 'enlightened common sense'.[44] He conceded that qualitative distinctions within this criterion could not be readily reduced to a common index. Nevertheless, he boldly asserted that 'a large and growing body of agreement would emerge, when a sufficient number of practical issues had been brought up for consideration', because 'the nature and the circumstances of mankind have so much in common, and the processes of civilisation are so powerfully assimilating them, as to furnish a continually increasing community of experience and feeling'.[45] Already 'a considerable amount of agreement exists among hygienists, educationalists, moralists, on matters of physical, intellectual and moral values'.[46] At any given time in history, there existed 'rules and standards of intellectual and moral, as of physical, well-being that express the general criteria of the best qualified judges'. [47]

His criterion of 'enlightened common sense' provided a rationale for a modern welfare state, and the role of experts within it, which was consistent with his notion of government as the 'brain' of the social organism, as noted in the previous chapter. He put great faith in experts, who could legitimately determine what was desirable, as opposed to the actually desired.

> In every organised society people are choosing not only for themselves how they will act, but for others, and often for others whom they seek

to influence 'for their good' against their immediate inclinations. Those in charge of children and other dependants, philanthropists, reformers, public administrators, exercise the right to overrule the current desires and tastes of their charges in favour of some higher standards.[48]

Choices made by authorities that overrode individual evaluations were only justified 'by assuming that the "best qualified" people have the right to impose standards of welfare, and that they can do so by virtue of some sort of consent or assent of the "government" [governed?]. All sound government rests upon these two assumptions, first that some persons are better qualified than others to determine values, secondly, that some recognition of this fact is generally acceded.'[49] People would tolerate such leadership because they 'will accept better standards than their own. All progress comes by assertion of initiative and leadership. Outstanding persons, or groups, thus impose a welfare that outstrips the current desires and approaches the desirable.'[50] He admitted that there were limitations to this view of accepting higher standards, but

> in spite of popular resentment of intellectual and moral 'swank', there is a growing acknowledgement alike by populace and Philistine of levels of thought and conduct somewhat higher than those in which they live. Most uneducated parents want some education for their children. As for moral standards, most people want to do 'right' most of the time, and accept and even profess ideals a little beyond their understanding and practice.[51]

The method

His method of evaluating human welfare, spelt out most fully in *Work and Wealth*, was a Ruskin-based variation of Bentham's 'felicific calculus'. He described his method as a 'New Utilitarianism', which brought qualitative and more complex psychological considerations into the calculus.[52]

Hobson's 'New Utilitarian', 'human economy' can be shown diagramatically:

Production	Wealth	Consumption
Art and exercise	Human utility	Needs
Labour		Abundance
Toil	Human cost	Satiety
Mal-production		Mal-consumption

Hobson, in explaining these categories, traced the aggregate of marketable goods and services backwards through the processes of their production and forwards into their consumption. Production could have its utilities and consumption its costs. 'Art' and 'exercise' were deemed creative or recreative and incurred no human cost. Hobson regarded 'labour' as rewarding because it was an expression of an individual's social being in terms of contributing to the collective good. On the consumption side, over and above the goods and services which contained utility in satisfying 'sound personal needs', there was 'abundance'. This possessed utility for it enabled the individual to 'contribute voluntarily to the good of others'.[53] As for human costs incurred in production, 'mal-production', which was 'bad and degrading in its nature', could arise, owing to an 'abuse of the creative faculty or of social control', and toil, which was excessive labour.[54] And within the consumption rubric 'satiety' was a cost, because unlike abundance it did not induce people to help others. There also existed mal-consumption, which resulted in 'poisonous reactions on personal and social welfare'.[55]

The object of this 'calculative' exercise was to achieve a 'human law of distribution' of work and consumption that maximised 'human utility' and minimised 'human cost'. This entailed, first, asking three questions about production: (1) what was the quality and kind of human effort involved in a business 'cost'? (2) what were the capacities of human beings who gave out these efforts?

(3) what was the distribution of effort among those who gave it out? Second, on the consumption side, what had to be known was: (1) the quality and kind of satisfaction or utility yielded by the good sold to the consumer; (2) the capacities of consumers to obtain utility; and (3) the distribution of these utilities among the con-suming public.[56]

The application

Hobson was more interested in attaching values to the various categories in his calculus than in developing a rigorous method of calculating human costs and satisfactions. He admitted that this involved an 'immense *petitio principii* [i.e. begging of the question]. The assumption of any close agreement as to the nature of individual well-being, still more social well-being, was logically quite unwarranted.'[57] But, as we have already noted, the 'working test' of 'enlightened common-sense' produced by common agree-ment would arise 'when a sufficient number of practical issues had been brought up for consideration'.[58] We can only assume that Hobson in applying his analysis was inspired by 'enlightened common-sense'!

How he assigned costs and utilities to different categories of producers and consumers can be dealt here only in outline. Artists – as did inventors – experienced few human costs, because they were undertaking creative work, but costs were entailed if they were compelled to repeat certain works or produce vulgar ones in order to cater for taste.[59] Professional workers were subjected to a mixture of costs and utilities since their work combined creativity with routine. The costs increasingly outweighed the utilities in the lower echelons of the professions. The jobs of industrial capitalists were creative, but there was a cost attached to risk-taking. Workers had to bear by far the largest costs of production. For them, work was totally uncreative, and was narrow, dull and repetitive, merely a means to an end.[60] The human costs of machine-minding in particular were high, in terms of physical and mental fatigue and illnesses.[61] Nevertheless, unlike Ruskin, he also stressed the actual and potentially liberating effects of machinery. It reduced the number of people who might otherwise have had to perform physically hard and monotonous jobs by hand, thereby creating the possibility of releasing them from dull jobs. Moreover, many jobs involving machinery could be interesting because they often required skill and judgement.[62]

Costs also arose from the way in which labour was distributed. Workers of equal capacities could be unequally burdened. And some could be periodically unemployed, while others not, or an individual could experience slack periods of working followed by excessive overtime.[63] Or people of unequal capacity could be subjected to equally onerous tasks, as when the very young, women or very old were forced to work as hard as able-bodied men.

Not only did work entail a cost; the production of capital did, too. For saving incurred a cost, either in the form of risk-taking or abstinence. Different classes of saver were affected in different ways. The rich incurred little cost because saving was automatic, the residue after all wants had been satisfied. The middle-class experienced little sacrifice since the abstinence involved was merely a postponement of consumption in order to purchase comforts or luxuries in the future.[64] A small element of risk, though, could be involved, thereby engendering a cost. Yet saving for the working class bore a real cost, since it often necessitated stinting on prime necessities.[65]

As for the human costs attached to consumption, Hobson contended that all social strata suffered from 'illth': 'A large proportion of the stimulants and drugs ... bad literature, art and recreations, the services of prostitutes and flunkeys, are conspicuous instances.'[66] Utility also depended upon the quantities consumed by the individual (e.g. whether they were sated or not), or whether they had the inherent, or acquired, capacity to derive maximum benefit from an article of consumption.[67]

Hobson then examined the amount of 'illth' contained in three types of consumption. There was the 'primary organic factor', essential to biological survival, shaped by the physical environment in which different people lived. Few costs were involved: 'The early evolution of a standard of necessary consumption, working under [the] close economy of trial and error appears to guarantee a free, natural instinctive selection of organically sound consumables.'[68] On the other hand, the 'industrial factor' of consumption, which entailed the 'modification of organic needs, due directly, or indirectly to conditions of work' were not cost-free.[69] Here, Hobson seemed to adopt the 'man-is-what-he eats' philosophy of the later Feuerbach.[70] The diet of those who performed heavy manual tasks 'may produce a coarse type of animalism, which precludes the formation of a higher nervous structure and the finer qualities of character that are its spiritual counterpart'.[71] Yet the consumption of sedentary brain-workers also had its disutilities: 'the physical abuses of athleticism, stimulants and drugs' and the 'fatuous or degrading forms of literature, drama, art, music'.[72]

Hobson was even more critical of those forms of consumption that fell within the category of the 'conventional factor', imposed by social custom. It involved indefinite amounts of waste and error: the damage of patent medicines, the 'arts' of adulteration and advertising, which created harmful and 'artificial' wants, and wastes amongst the poorer classes through imitating the upper classes, involving such things as bad clothing and gambling. But for Hobson the upper classes themselves were responsible for the largest amount of bad consumption: their conspicuous consumption that was engendered by their quest for personal distinction in order to impress others, the 'futile' waste manifest in their social duties, the 'idle round of visits' and entertainments. The largest source of 'injurious waste' accrued from recreation, education and charity. Sport in particular was a harmful form of recreation, since it diverted 'into lower forms of activity the zests and interests intended to promote a life of work and art',[73] and it spoiled 'the spontaneity and liberty of play, which is a necessity of every life'.[74] Education could be regarded as a disutility because studies were 'valued more highly as decorative accomplishments than as utilities, as evidenced in the study of dead languages'.[75] History and literature were treated not in relation to life, 'but as dead matter'.[76] And charity was not genuine but the product of a false piety and of the huge, immorally gained, surpluses that the rich possessed.

Explaining the malady: the surplus

The unproductive surplus

Hobson's explanation of this physical, mental and moral waste, in all its productive and consumptive forms, followed directly from his organic evolutionary perspective in which the growth of a 'surplus energy' over and above that required for physical survival assumed critical importance. His concept of surplus also clearly revealed what he saw as lacking in orthodox political economy, the absence of a specifically ethical dimension, and of a unifying explanatory framework.

Before looking more closely at the function of the surplus concept within his 'system', its actual meaning requires brief consideration, in the light of John Allett's overall interpretation of Hobson. He sees what he describes as the 'theory of organic surplus value' as the linchpin of Hobson's political and economic philosophy.[77] Allett rests his thesis on a passage from *The Social Problem*.[78] In it, Hobson argues that the surplus could not be attributable to any single worker, but was the product of the co-operation between workers. As he states: 'Organised co-operation is a productive power.'[79] If workers were set to work 'firstly separately and then together, the difference in value between their added and their joint product might rank as the quantity of social value'.[80] This definition has prompted Allett to charge other commentators with failing to see the surplus as intrinsic to capitalism, and with mistakenly assuming that for Hobson the industrial system would be morally and economically healthy if freed of monopoly control.[81] Allett, on the contrary, holds that Hobson believed that capitalism 'even at its most ideal' was an unjust system of distribution.[82]

There are, however, a number of serious flaws with such a perspective. The first is that Allett misinterprets the context of the passage upon which he relies so heavily. All Hobson was seeking to do was to demonstrate the social character of the productive process, in order to establish that society had 'a natural claim upon property, on the ground that it is the maker of values of property'.[83] In other words, this notion of surplus was merely part of an argument seeking to justify a general claim by the state upon individual property. Because property was a social, and not an individual, product individual rights over it could not be absolute. The fact that he did not endow this form of surplus with explanatory or normative-distributive significance, or make it into a full-blown theory within his overall system, is confirmed by the paucity of references to it in previous or later works. This paucity could be explained by the fact that Hobson's purpose was to unite liberal and socialist values, or individual and collective ones. A theory of 'organic surplus' could not deal with the question of individual entitlements.

Secondly, the surplus that commentators criticised by Allett are refering to is, what Hobson called, an 'industrial surplus', which he closely linked to machine production.[84] With the advent of industrialism, a surplus was created over and above that required for the means of subsistence, which Hobson saw as the equivalent to the amount required to 'maintain the current output of

63

productive energy in a factor of production', i.e. the surplus was the amount left after subsistence payments had been made to the factors of production required as an incentive to maintain an existing level of output.[85] Thus, machine production was the decisive factor in creating physical resources in excess of those required for physical subsistence, rather than the act of co-operation itself. True, co-operation could be seen as a necessary condition for the creation of the surplus in developing machine production, but it was the latter which was the crucial physical agency. And, as we have seen in the previous chapter, it was this growth of human productivity that enabled both society and the individual to 'realise' themselves. Thirdly, because he used the notion of an 'industrial' surplus, he did, *contra* Allett, on a number of occasions suggest that *laissez-faire*, pre-industrial, pre-monopoly capitalism was, by and large, just. For in this situation a 'needs' economy operated, in which all factors of production received their appropriate payment for maintainence.[86] Finally, if Allett's in-terpretation were accepted, it would have had a peculiar logic for Hobson. If the 'organic' surplus demonstrated that capitalism was intrinsically unjust, then he should call for its destruction rather than its reform. For Hobson, the inequity of capitalism lay in the market process, rather than in production itself. And here, as we shall see in the final chapter, he was decidedly equivocal about whether such a process under capitalism was inherently unfair. Thus, all that can be said for the 'organic' theory of surplus value is that it helped strengthen Hobson's case against those who insisted that individual property rights were absolute.

What we may call an 'industrial-incentive' surplus concept played a much more important explanatory and normative role within Hobson's overall theorising. In an unreformed, industrial capitalist system, much of this surplus, generated by industrial machine production, was 'unproductive',[87] in the sense that it consisted of 'payments [in the form of rent, excessive interest,

profit or salary] to owners of factors of production as evoke no ...
increase of product'.[88] Much of the surplus accrued to the
monopoly capitalists who were primarily located in industries that
relied heavily on machine production. These capitalists had a strong
bargaining position vis-à-vis the worker and consumer.

The surplus, in its 'unproductive' form, was responsible for all
capitalism's defects. 'When this [unproductive] surplus income is
traced, backward to the human costs involved in its production,
forward to the human injuries inflicted by the excessive and bad
consumption it sustains, it is seen to be the direct efficient cause
of all the human defects in our economic system.'[89] Since most of
it went to the wealthy, it was devoted to luxury and 'illth', thereby
reducing the quantum of human welfare rather than increasing it.
Additionally, since this leisured class did not work, a loss of
production resulted. And the rest of the population tended to copy
them in their injurious or wasteful consumer habits.[90] The expenditure of the surplus in this fashion also led workers to perform
'futile, frivolous, vicious or servile tasks'.[91] Furthermore, the actual
production of the surplus entailed speed-ups and long hours for
workers. Significantly, it could have a reverse effect: in Hobson's
eyes it was the root cause of economic depression, of
underconsumption.

> The absence of any rational security for the apportionment of surplus
> will be seen to be the chief cause in producing those trade fluctuations
> which bring periods of unemployment and under-employment to large
> masses of productive resources thereby deprived of their wages of
> subsistence.[92]

This thesis, for which Hobson is famous, will be the focus of the
next section. Finally, the conflict that arose over the distribution
of the surplus was considered by Hobson as the chief obstacle to
the creation of a socially harmonious society: 'In origin, as they
emerge in rents, profiteering, and other price extortions, they

evoke hostility and struggle between capital and labour, landlord and tenant, producer and consumer, and between the various trades and labour groupings in their dealings with one another.'[93] Thus, to put the matter succinctly, the key function of a state with increased social and economic responsibilities should be the transformation of the surplus, so that it became 'productive' rather than 'unproductive'. This will be considered in the following chapter.

In one sense, Hobson's concept of surplus was not new. It originated in Ricardo's notion of economic rent, which consisted of unearned income accruing to land ownership, and whose size depended upon the diminishing fertility of the soil (termed 'differential rent'). The idea was given great publicity as a result of the barnstorming campaigns of the American Henry George in the 1880s, who eloquently advocated a 'Single Tax' on the unearned increment, specifically accruing to land ownership, as an all-embracing panacea for social problems. The Liberals' Unauthorised Programme of 1885, promulgated by Joseph Chamberlain and others, distinguished between earned and unearned incomes. The Fabians extended the concept of rent to other factor incomes, apart from land.[94] Hobson followed them in this, but did not see its origins primarily in differential terms, i.e. as the result of superior abilities, or of superior land or capital. Rather, he concentrated on demonstrating that it arose from market processes. Even 'perfect' markets, the working assumption of orthodox economists, created surpluses. 'Consumer' and 'producer' surpluses accrued to both buyers and sellers at any given price. This occurred because at that price some suppliers would be prepared to supply the same quantity of goods even at a lower price, and some purchasers would have been prepared to buy the same quantity at a higher price. Both these groups therefore received 'windfalls'.[95]

Yet Hobson was much more interested in showing how

economic rent or 'unearned surpluses' were derived from contingent imperfections in the market. For example, the limited numbers of buyers and sellers and the indivisibility of goods fixed an upper and lower price limit and this meant that force or cunning determined the final price.[96] Unfair advantages could also be gained through naturally or artificially induced scarcity, and, equally significant, the time factor could be an important price determinant. Sellers of perishable goods, especially labour, were in a hurry to sell. This enabled capitalists to exploit their superior bargaining position by withholding employment. The power of capital 'rests on the fact that the sale of labour power involves the purchase of the right to live; the power to starve labour into submission still survives as the final economic arbiter'.[97] Thus, capital naturally had the upper hand, a position further strengthened if it was in a monopolistic (or, in more correct economic jargon, 'monopsonistic') situation *vis-à-vis* labour. Although he recognised that unearned surpluses were contained in rents, dividends, and interest, as a result of unfair bargains, he implicitly assumed that the largest surplus derived from the wage-bargain.[98] It was 'the heaviest ethical indictment of the economic system'.[99] Indeed, his notion of the 'unearned' or 'unproductive' surplus – it is significant how he used these terms interchangeably, although literally they could be taken to mean different things – is the clearest example of his attempt to show how economic facts had an ethical dimension. The 'unearned surplus' was morally abhorrent because it stemmed from cunning or force and not honest toil. It caused the economy to malfunction, through underconsumption, and, in creating an idle social strata, it was 'unproductive'.

Hobson and Marxist economics

At this juncture, Hobson's differences with Marxist economic theory can be recorded, since it, too, has a theory of 'surplus'.

67

Before doing so, we can also note that he levelled much broader criticisms against Marxism. Until the last two years of his life, he remained convinced that it could have little appeal in Britain.[100] It would not be able to root itself in British working-class culture, which had little respect for intellectual authority and was opposed to 'extreme' measures.[101] Its dismissal of religion also helped diminish its influence. It could not tap into people's moral energies, which were often inspired by religious belief.[102] Moreover, although its 'emotional blend of combativeness and humanity' might possess a certain resonance amongst a number of 'thoughtful workers', it could not for rational 'free' thinkers.[103] Furthermore, it was strategically flawed as a result of its demand to equalise all incomes. This alienated potential support amongst the enlightened capitalist and middle classes, whom Hobson regarded as crucial in any movement for 'progressive' social change.[104] At a more philosophical level, he asserted that the 'dialectic' was an 'empty intellectual paradox'[105] and that Marxism suffered from an excess of economic determinism in reducing the explanation of most social phenomena to the economic.[106] Nevertheless, despite his many unfavourable comments, he did come to recognise that Marx, in his analysis of trade depressions and imperialism, had anticipated him.[107]

Hobson's more specific and technical criticisms were directed against Marx's economic analysis, especially his theory of value and surplus value. In terms reminiscent of Bernstein's critique of Marxism in *Evolutionary Socialism*, he saw the labour theory of value grounded upon a false abstractionism, akin to marginalist theory, which reduced qualitative differences to quantitative ones, especially in transforming the value of skilled labour to units of simple, unskilled labour time, 'a common measure which could never operate in actual industry'.[108] Rather dubiously, he also argued that the theory implied an acceptance of the existing system of wealth distribution, because Marx justified his reductionist assumption by asserting that it was a 'social process that goes on behind the backs of the producers'. This was 'to accept the respective valuations this "social process" assigns to the different sorts of human effort'.[109] Thus, for example, a highly skilled surgeon deserved much higher remuneration than a labourer, because this differential could be explained in terms of a multiple of 'simple labour'. Hobson further maintained that this reductionism undermined Marx's theory of surplus value, presumably in the sense that capitalists were justified in receiving higher rewards than workers, owing to their greater skills.[110] His final objection was that the theory separated value from price. His own theory, derived from Alfred Marshall's, equated price with value.

> Nearly the whole trouble with value has arisen from separating unduly the consideration of value from that of price. Once keep clearly in [mind?] the fundamental truth that price is value in terms of money, it will then appear that the most profitable way of studying the nature of value is to study the forces which cause price-change.[111]

Thus, value was determined by the interaction of cost and utility.[112]

The market framework not only formed the basis of his own theory of value but also his notion of 'surplus value'. Surpluses could arise out of all bargains in the market-place, and could accrue to any factor of production, depending on their relative bargaining strength, their 'pull'. Accordingly, Marx, in not understanding the significance of bargaining activities, was wrong, according to Hobson, in seeing surplus value as exclusively the product of labour power taken by capital in the process of bargaining for the sale of labour power. He failed to explain why labour alone of the productive factors, should be conceived as making all the 'value' of material marketable goods. Further, he was unable to explain what the nature of that power was by which capital took the surplus value made by labour; and, finally, he was unable to show how any individual capitalist who took surplus value from workers was not compelled to relinquish it as a result of competition with other capitalists.[113]

Underconsumption

At this stage Hobson's underconsumptionist theory warrants mention, as one of the effects of the imperfect market mechanism. Although the theory was biographically significant for Hobson in making him a 'heretic', he regarded his exposure of the inequities of the market as his most 'destructive heresy'.[114] And although he devoted a considerable energy to convincing others of the veracity of his underconsumptionist theory, it was for him merely one effect of the 'unproductive' surplus, and only one element within his 'organic' socio-economic philosophy.

In holding to his underconsumptionist thesis, he rejected one of the central tenets of economic orthodoxy, which asserted that oversaving (i.e. overinvestment for Hobson) was an impossibility. According to Say's Law, supply created its own demand, so that all that was produced was consumed. All payments made in the form of costs of production were used to consume all that had been produced in a given period. Thus capitalism, in theory at least, was a self-equilibriating system. For Hobson, on the contrary, there existed an imbalance between saving (i.e. investment) and spending. Initially, along with A. F. Mummery, he attributed this to an individual, psychological phenomenon, to the 'undue exercise of the habit of saving'.[115] He later attributed oversaving to a maldistribution of the surplus, which was at bottom a moral problem:

> My proposition is that the existence of a 'surplus' income not earned by its recipients and not applying any normal stimulus to industry, has the effect of disturbing the economical adjustment between spending and saving, and of bringing about those periodical congestions and stoppages of industry with which we are familiar.[116]

Individuals attempted to invest in more capital than was socially required, because 'they possess certain elements of income which are not earned by effort, and which are therefore not required to satisfy any present legitimate wants' for 'no class of men whose "savings" are made out of their hard-won earnings is likely to oversave, for each unit of "capital" will represent a real want, a piece of legitimate consumption deferred.'[117] Saving for the wealthy, therefore, was an automatic process, not pursued to gratify any future consumption needs. As a consequence, these savings were channelled into the production of capital goods, in excess of the amount required to satisfy future effective demand.

He outlined the sequence of events that led to crisis in the following way:

> Our saving class is … not necessarily causing increase of 'employment' by paying workers to put up more factories instead of using their moneys to demand consumables. So long as the 'saving' is actually in progress – i.e. so long as the factory and machinery are being made, – the net employment of the community is just as large as if the money were spent to demand commodities; more labour is engaged in making factories, less in working them. But after the new factories are made, they can only be worked on condition that there is an increase of consumption correspondent to the increase of producing power – i.e. on the condition that a sufficient number of persons are actuated by motives different from those which animated the 'saving' class, and will consent to give validity to the saving of the former by 'spending' on commodities an increased proportion of their incomes. Where no such expectation is realized, an attempt to 'operate' the new factories does not give any net increase in employment, it only gluts the markets, drives down prices, closes the weaker factories, imparts irregularity of work, and generally disorganizes trade.[118]

Thus, for the economy to work smoothly there had to exist a definite quantitative relation between the rate of production and the rate of consumption, between 'saving' and spending.

Whatever the technical merits of the theory, we can note here Hobson's tenacity throughout his intellectual career in criticising alternative explanations of unemployment, as well as defending his own thesis, especially towards the end of his life. Over the years he explicitly rejected various theories of unemployment and economic depression that came into vogue. Naturally, he criticised the individualistic explanation that unemplyment stemmed from moral imperfections: 'Personal causes do not to any appreciable extent cause unemployment, but largely determine who shall be unemployed.'[119] He also dismissed the theory advanced by Jevons that depression was mainly attributable to poor wheat harvests – the result of sunspots – if only because statistics showed no correspondence between changes in the world production of wheat and fluctuations in employment.[120] Nor did he consider the introduction of machinery as a crucial cause. Although technological innovation could account for a constant percentage of unemployment over the long term, there was little reason to assume that it was responsible for periods of generally depressed trade.[121]

As for monetary explanations, he denied, for example, that a shortage of gold led to a general fall in prices and therefore trade depression. The facts did not tally. One proof that gold was scarce was that it was supposed to be accompanied by high interest rates, but these usually coincided with high prices.[122] Neither could he agree that the shrinkage of credit could be a plausible explanation: the banks in withdrawing credit were merely responding to an objective situation – a shrinkage of markets.[123] In addition, he did not believe that interest rates would naturally maintain the correct ratio between saving and spending. Interest rates could not regulate large sources of saving – new capital raised by public bodies through taxation, or by firms from internal reserves. And the savings of the wealthy were automatic.[124] Finally, a theory with which he did have some sympathy, because it contained an underconsumptionist element, was the Douglas 'social credit' hypothesis. This saw depressions as stemming from the inability of aggregate demand to absorb current production, because the money represented in wages, salaries, etc. that had been paid to the producers of current output had for the most part already been spent on consumption before these goods had reached the retailer. Hence, the need for 'social credit'. Hobson looked at the process from the opposite direction: current production was absorbed by those who had been paid to produce future stocks.[125]

Hobson's own underconsumptionist theory only came under serious academic scrutiny, especially from Keynes and his followers in the Labour Party, such as Evan Durbin, in Britain during the 1920s and 1930s,[126] as his views were gaining wider currency within the labour movement. The crux of their criticism was that he erroneously equated saving with investment, which had led him to argue that economic crises were caused by the failure of increased investment to be absorbed by increased consumption. Keynes, on the contrary, held that crises could be avoided by increased investment. Recessions were the product of underinvestment, the result of the growth of idle bank balances, i.e. 'liquidity preference'.[127] The solution could either be an increase in consumption – and here Keynes agreed with Hobson – or investment, his prefered remedy because of the 'multiplier effect'.[128]

His defence amounted to little more than a reiteration of his position and an insistence that idle bank balances were merely an effect of unsuitable investment outlets, resulting from previous overinvestment.[129] His refusal to make any concessions to his critics was quite understandable for intellectual, moral and ideological reasons.[130] It was part of his attempt to develop a systemic economic framework that contained a unifying explanatory hypothesis, as well as combining empirical analysis and normative prescription, with the concept of 'surplus' at its centre. And to advocate alternative explanations avoided questioning what he held to be the moral basis of the socio-economic malaise. For Hobson, as for Ruskin, 'life without work is robbery',[131] and the 'unearned' surplus which caused economic disequilibria was therefore at root a moral problem: 'Our main economic troubles are of distinctively moral origin.'[132] Thus, to have advocated different solutions to unemployment would have been to accept the continued existence of social parasitism.

Conclusion

We have seen in this chapter the importance of Ruskin's and Hobson's own perspectives in providing a humanistic criterion as a basis from which to criticise both orthodox political economy and the capitalist system itself. The former in its obsession with marketable wealth, failed to recognise the imperative of meeting real human needs, and the latter in an unreformed state could not satisfy them. For his own ethical and economic analysis, his concept of surplus, particularly in its 'industrial' connotation, was crucial. It had a central unifying role within theory and practice. Firstly, it enabled him to unite his philosophical, evolutionary theory with his economic theory. The growth of the surplus throughout human history created the material basis for the increased possibilities of 'individuation', and for changing the shape of human needs, from the quantitative to the qualitative. It was the ultimate purpose of political economy to suggest ways in which the surplus could be created and distributed as efficiently as possible. Within the realms of economic theory, this meant the 'reform' rather than the rejection of orthodox political economy, because he accepted that all factors of production were entitled to a payment required to maintain and enhance their productivity. He wanted merely to strip these factors of payments that were in excess of the amount required to keep them functioning 'progressively', in order to bring about greater 'individuation'. His notion of surplus also enabled him to develop a unifying explanation for the laws of distribution. It moreover assisted him in unifying the 'is' and the 'ought' missing from conventional economic theory. It was the key explanation of capitalism's malfunction, and it was a true moral measure of what was wrong with it – poverty amidst plenty, the idleness and wastefulness of the rich, and the 'sweating' or enforced idleness of the poor. The concept had a further unifying role, to which we turn in the next chapter. It connected his economic with his political theory, underpinning his demand for broadening the state's economic function.

4 Between liberalism and socialism

Hobson sought to reapportion the surplus according to a set of principles firmly set within an 'organic' framework and reconstituted political economy. This entailed a redrawing of the boundaries between the state and society, avoiding the extremes of individualist liberalism and, what he saw as, collectivist socialism. Yet, he wanted to incorporate the virtues of both ideologies.[1] Thus, in analysing their respective theories of human nature, for example, he endorsed the traditional liberal respect for individuality and the need to acknowledge human differences. Nevertheless, he could not fully accept the existence of unqualified human egoism as a fixed datum. Through education, people could become more 'other-regarding',[2] or self-sacrificing, a quality he associated more with a socialist view of human nature. However, self-sacrifice could not be unlimited. There remained an irrevocably selfish element in human nature that had to be recognised and harnessed to the community through the use of incentives.[3] At the same time, he accepted the socialist argument that unlimited acquisitiveness was anti-social and immoral. As we shall see, he made the socialist distributional formula 'From each according to his powers, to each according to his needs' his own, although he introduced an incentive element.

Equally, Hobson rejected extreme individualist, or socialist remedies to the 'Social Problem'. For instance, he opposed the temperance solution, widely advocated within the Liberal Party in the 1890s and earlier. He concluded from his underconsumptionist analysis of economic fluctuations that even if an outburst of sobriety occurred, the periodic over-stocking of the labour market would still continue. The issue of drink was relevant only in the sense that it might determine who was to be made unemployed in the first instance.[4]

He reserved, however, his greatest critical animus for the nostrum of individual charity, championed by the Charity Organisation (COS). Its philosophy was articulated by Bernard Bosanquet, also a major influence within the London Ethical Society, of which Hobson was a member in the early 1890s. Looking at his objections to Bosanquet's doctrines, we can understand his reasons for leaving the Society. Indeed, given that his basic, anti-philanthropic position had been worked out by 1891 in *Problems of Poverty*, it is surprising that he remained a member of the Society for so long.[5] If his objective had been to win the Society around to a more collectivist position, it would seem that he had given up hope by 1896. He launched a ferocious attack on the COS in his article entitled 'The Social Philosophy of Charity Organisation'.[6]

His critique of the Organisation's moral individualism, with its avoidance of socio-economic explanations of, and collectivist solutions to, poverty, revealed his characteristically ill-concealed outrage at upper-class hypocrisy. The COS held that state 'doles' for the unemployed, poor and needy undermined their capacities for sound citizenship, and therefore their ability to formulate adequately a 'general will' as members of society. 'Doles' 'derationalised' people by detaching effort from enjoyment, and by destroying the incentive to work, individual responsibility and family solidarity. State aid made them dependent, apathetic creatures, unable and unwilling to plan and realise their own futures. The answer according to the COS lay in the private, individual charity of social work, which relied heavily on moral instruction. This would build up the 'character' of the 'client'. Indeed, for the COS, the prerequisite of social reform was the reform of individual 'character'. This was the 'condition of conditions'.[7]

For Hobson, on the other hand, the attribution of poverty to the defects of individual character conveniently deflected criticism away from the social structure:

> the philosophy which finds the only momentum of social reform in the moral energy of the individual members of the masses is just the smart sophistry which the secret self-interest of the comfortable classes has always been weaving in order to avoid important and inconvenient searching into the foundations of social inequality.[8]

This sophistry also manifested itself in the COS's highly selective condemnation of the unworked-for doles of the poor. Why was this analysis not applied to the 'doles' of the rich, who gained their wealth through inheritance or the 'pulls' of the market?[9] Thus, given the highly dubious origins of the rich's wealth, the real moral problem lay not with the poor but with the rich, whose strong position in the market created a stratum of needy people.[10]

His economic analysis additionally led him to reject the COS assumption that the overcoming of poverty was a matter of morality and willpower. Like the argument of the temperance reformers, who attributed unemployment to drinking habits, this confused 'any' with 'all'. Owing to the existence of trade flucutations, not 'all' could be employed, but 'any' individual might be able to get work.[11]

Finally, Hobson employed the biological elements of his organic perspective to undermine the proposition that moral reform was a prerequisite of citizenship and the realisation of a general will, and that state aid was an obstacle to citizenship. He turned the argument on its head. He appealed to the notion of a 'hierarchy of needs'. Material conditions were a necessary, though not sufficient, factor in bringing about the 'moral elevation' of the poor. He had developed this position somewhat earlier, when he drew inspiration from Aristotle's dictum: 'It is needful first to have a maintenance, and then practice virtue.'[12] Hobson asserted that: 'So long as the bare struggle for existence absorbs all their energies, [people] cannot be civilized ... We must begin with the lower life before we can ascend to the higher.'[13] And material conditions could only be improved through a collectivist programme. He turned the COS argument on its head in another sense: the state reform of the social structure, far from being a hindrance to the general will, was indeed an expression of its very essence, of its necessarily communal intent.[14]

At the other end of the spectrum he rejected, although in not such fierce tones, 'full theoretic Socialism', which he identified with total state control over production, distribution and exchange in order to achieve egalitarian ends.[15] First, as we have already noted, such a system ignored the importance of individual incentives in the form of 'prize-money', integral to economic progress.[16] Secondly, the abolition of the market in allocating work and consumption, and its replacement by a planning system, would ignore different subjective preferences between people in relation to work and consumption. For example, in coping with distribution, such a system would have difficulty in allocating products on the basis of different individual capacities to enjoy them, or according to different tastes. Moreover, in so far as a socialist system forced all to perform minimum routine services for the community, it would not be taking into account differing individual capacities and wills to do such work.[17] The fact that socialism ignored individual differences also led him to reject Shaw's egalitarian proposal that all citizens should have equal incomes: people had different abilities to gain benefit from a given quantity of money. Thus, equal distribution would be inefficient in terms of the maximisation of individual satisfactions from a given income.[18] As opposed to 'theoretical socialism', he advocated 'practicable socialism'[19] through the state promotion of economic equality of opportunity in the market-place, which would result in supplying 'all workers at cost price with all the economic conditions requisite to the education and employment of their personal powers for their personal advantage and enjoyment.'[20]

Distributing the surplus

The way in which he proposed to redistribute the 'unproductive' surplus clearly illustrates his endeavour to avoid the extremes of individualism and collectivism, and yet retain what he saw as valuable in both ideologies. He wanted to ensure that his proposals for state intervention would respect the heterogeneity as well as the homogeneity of human needs, desires and capacities, whilst simultaneously satisfying the 'needs' of society seen as an 'organic' whole.

The state

The state as much as the individual was entitled to consume some of the surplus. We have already noted in Chapter two the general argument in support of the state's right to make such a claim: the surplus was a social product, and the state, as representative of society, could legitimately use it for the benefit of society as a whole. Hobson, however, offered specific grounds for justifying the expenditure of the 'three great departments of the "public good"', 'health, education and security'.[21] The purpose of these forms of public expenditure were fourfold. First, 'the improvement of the conditions of life' was 'essential to the stability and progress of industry'.[22] By this Hobson meant the creation of a healthier and better educated and therefore more 'efficient' workforce. Second, such outlay was designed to promote equality of opportunity in a double sense. In a procedural, competitive sense, a free education system would promote greater equality of opportunity, for example, within the civil service.[23] And it would generally reduce rents of ability that arise out of skills shortages.[24] Public expenditure would, moreover, foster equality of opportunity in a substantive sense, in creating an environment in which all could 'individuate'.[25] Finally, he saw it as an expression of the 'self-realisation of society'. He made a contrast between public squalor and private affluence, and asked: 'Are [England's] streets, its public buildings, worthy expressions of a rich and civilised community?'[26]

The individual: the 'human economy'

The principle that underlay the distribution of the unproductive surplus for individuals was in accord with his 'New Utilitarianism', his Ruskin-inspired, revised version of Bentham's felicific calculus. It was a 'human economy' designed 'to distribute Wealth in relation to its production on the one hand and its consumption on the other, in order to secure the minimum of Human Costs and the maximum of Human Utility.'[27] Put simply, this meant for Hobson the creation of more, but not unlimited, objective wealth as efficiently as possible with the least human cost, and from which the greatest satisfaction was derived.

The most important distributive principle for apportioning the surplus was contained in the socialist maxim 'From each according to his powers, to each according to his needs'.[28] Yet his definition of 'needs' clearly revealed his desire to fuse liberal and socialist principles. Thus, on the liberal side, he accepted that the requirements of production determined 'needs', in a double sense. First, membership of a productive category established the type of 'need' that an individual possessed, and therefore the form of reward to which they were entitled as an incentive to maintain, and indeed, improve their productive function. Since Hobson endorsed the productive categories of liberal political economy, and their attendant rewards (albeit in modified form), he took it for granted that an individual could be productive either through contributing savings, making capital or by offering labour. And for these efforts the individual was entitled to rewards in the form of interest, profit and wages. To these rewards, where they were justified, he gave the generic term 'property', and where they were unearned, and therefore illegitimate, 'improperty'. Thus, his objective was not to abolish the existing forms of reward, except for rent derived from land, when it was not part of the 'wear-and-tear' fund. Rather, he wanted to put 'property' on an ethical basis: 'When all Property is visibly justified, alike in origin and use, the rights of property will for the first time be respected because they will be for the first time respectable.'[29] In reforming the distributive categories he hoped to restore the harmony between these factors, a *modus vivendi* he believed characteristic of pre-monopolistic phase of capitalism. This, he believed, lasted for most of the nineteenth century, when an 'unseen, unconscious harmony of selfish interests … sustained the industrial system and provided fairly effective government …'.[30] Indeed, he maintained that principles of efficiency and equity that underlay a competitive *laissez-faire* economy accorded with his distributional formula. The problem was that these principles could not be realised under modern conditions of industrial combination, both of capitalists and workers, although principally the former.[31] Perfect competition was no longer possible.

Those elements parasitically accruing to the different factors of production he wished to eradicate through state action can be seen in his discussion of his proposed distinction between 'maintenance', 'productive surplus' and 'unproductive surplus'.

Unproductive Surplus (unearned increment) C
Productive Surplus (costs of growth) B
Maintenance (costs of subsistence) A
A. Maintenance includes (1) minimum wages for various sorts of labour and ability necessary to support and evoke their continuous output at the present standard of efficiency; (2) depreciation or wear and tear of plant and other fixed capital; (3) minimum interest necessary to support the 'saving' involved in the production and

maintenance of the existing fabric of capital; (4) a 'wear-and-tear' provision for land.

B. The productive surplus includes (1) minimum wage of progressive efficiency in quantity and quality of labour and ability of various grades; (2) such rise of interest above the subsistence rate as is required to evoke and maintain the increase of saving required for industrial progress.

C. The unproductive surplus consists of (1) economic rent of land and other natural resources; (2) all interest beyond the rate involved in A and B; (3) all profit, salaries, or other payments for ability or labour in excess of what is economically necessary to evoke the sufficient use of such factor of production.[32]

Hobson's liberalism was not only displayed in his assumption that an individual's needs, and hence rewards, were governed by membership of a general, productive category within a capitalist framework. It possessed a second distributive characteristic: he redescribed 'needs' in such a way that recognised individual differences in productive ability, consistent with the value he attached to 'efficient' labour and industrial progress. People were not to be paid according to 'needs' in the conventional sense of what might be appropriate to satisfy their needs as multi-faceted human beings, with all sorts of physical, emotional, intellectual, aesthetic and creative requirements, but according to their productive ability.[33] He understood 'needs' to consist of 'the satisfaction of those physical, intellectual, and moral wants which serve to maintain and raise individual efficiency for social service'. Only by the satisfaction of such neeeds could an individual be kept in a position to serve society 'by efficient labour "according to his powers"'.[34]

Since human capacities and capabilities were different, Hobson envisaged inequalities of income. Thus, at the crudest level, a larger output of physical energy required a larger replacement through consumption, and therefore greater remuneration.[35] But, in his discussion of differentials between different categories of skill, he was far from stipulating that a navvy should receive more than a manager. With the latter category 'we have to deal with a class of worker whose social efficiency demands continual progress in the development of his mental and moral powers. The necessity of this development imposes more needs upon the worker.' Thus, 'social utility' demanded that these 'needs' should be met, and since society could not monitor each 'each several need' as it arose, the 'high-grade' worker had to have a higher rate of pay than a 'low-grade' worker, because his 'needs' were greater. And since these 'needs' could be properly supplied only by private expenditure, 'he ought to have a larger property'.[36] For example: 'Professional men and other brain workers may have a ... complex standard of needs, corresponding to the greater delicacy of their work.' Therefore, their income had to 'furnish more seclusion in the home, books and other private apparatus, opportunities for travel and wide inter-course'.[37]

This 'needs' formula of distribution he justified in organic terms. It was 'the organic law of distribution as applicable to the industrial organism as the animal organism'.[38] That the individual human 'cell' of society required nourishment for growth and survival was analogous to the needs of a cell within a biological organism. And since each cell or group of cells had different functions, so their 'needs' were different.[39] Furthermore, just as a disabled part of the organism required 'a larger supply of food and other organic defence placed at its disposal', so the needs of the young, old, sick, the 'mentally or morally defective, and the unemployed' had to be met 'not with reference to the current powers they exercise, but by an educative, curative, or preventive policy, directed, either to secure for society the use of their future powers, or to enable society to bear more easily a burden which it cannot shed'.[40]

Hobson accepted human differences in another sense. He was prepared to allow the talented but selfish person a differential payment on grounds of social utility.

> A selfish man with a real individual superiority of skill over his fellow craftsman will be able to take a larger reward and so long as he insists upon receiving his larger reward as a condition of doing his full and best work, it ranks as an individual economic 'need'. This will continue to be a basis of inequality of property.[41]

He came to recognise that this 'injuriously compromise[d] the principle of distribution according to needs'[42] in contrast to his earlier position.[43] Nevertheless, his distributive formula could be seen as corresponding to Marx's account of the first stage of communism in the *Critique of the Gotha Programme,* when the 'bourgeois right' of incentives still prevailed.[44]

Finally, he took note of individual differences in a way that could effectively run counter to his needs/productivity theory of distribution.[45] He suggested that income should be distributed according to an individual's ability to gain maximum utility from it. 'The needs of people, their capacity to get utility out of incomes by consuming it, are no more equal than their powers of production. Neither in respect of food, or clothing, or the general material standard of comfort, can any such equality of needs be alleged.'[46] Nevertheless, the key criterion for differentials lay in unequal productive abilities.

Hobson, however, had no intention of justifying *existing* inequalities of income, containing as they often did an 'unearned' surplus element. Moreover, he constantly argued that generally, and within limits, higher wages would lead to greater productive efficiency through improved health and morale.[47]

A minimum wage

Whilst he strongly advocated differential rewards, he also upheld a notion of needs, more closely identified with the socialist tradition. He urged that all adults were entitled to a minimum standard of life, as a result of their 'common humanity', which necessitated 'an adequate provision of food, shelter, health, education and other prime necessaries of life, so as to yield equal satisfaction of such requirements to all members of the community...'.[48] Thus, his demand for a minimum wage could be seen as part of his 'New Utilitarian' calculus of increasing aggregate utility, both in terms of consumption (i.e. similar types and amounts of commodities going to individuals and their families because they had similar needs, and could therefore derive equal amounts of satisfaction from them), and in terms of production (i.e. in creating a healthier and more productive workforce.[49] But this minimum was also part of his wider project of moral reform. It would nurture 'the life and health of the family, and that sense of security which is essential to sound character and regular habits, to the exercise of foresight, and the formation and execution of reasonable plans'.[50] In pressing for a national minimum, Hobson combined liberal and socialist principles in recognising human differences and similarities. Upon this minimum income inequality was built, 'adjusted to the specific needs of any class or group whose work or physical conditions marks it out as different from others'.[51] Thus, differentials between different productive groups, and within them, were legitimate.

Equality of opportunity

Hobson, in wishing to reduce existing inequalities, not only proposed what he saw as the socialist demand for a minimum wage. The liberal demand for equality of opportunity, in its competitive sense, also had a pivotal function. It would help reduce the unearned surplus derived from, for example, rents of ability.[52] He further held that legislation which improved working conditions strengthened workers' bargaining position *vis-à-vis* capital therefore increased their opportunities to obtain a larger share of the surplus.[53] Finally, he justified the principle on the utilitarian ground of greater efficiency. It stimulated productive talents that would otherwise have been wasted.[54]

Yet he did not believe that the demand was based upon an absolute or self-sufficient principle. Just as he urged that equal political rights did not make everybody fit to govern, because people had varying abilities, so he felt that equality of economic opportunity could not be mechanically applied.[55] Access to resources should be dependent on the ability to use them.[56] Equally crucial, it was too individualistic as an all-embracing principle. Although it could dissipate the surplus, it gave no guarantee that human resources would be used in the best way. A policy designed to use economic resources for the enrichment of human life had to be 'socially conceived and administered', because 'in origin and utilisation, these resources and the activities that employ them are social, and society is something more and other than an aggregate of individuals co-operating for purely individual ends'.[57] Hence, there was a need for some sort of social planning.

Production and consumption: the 'organic' connection

Hobson's felicific calculus sought not only to reduce the disutilities of work and increase the utilities of consumption for the individual and the collectivity. He saw a crucial 'organic' connection between production and consumption. Individuals were both producers and consumers. Thus, a crucial link existed, for example, between an individual's working conditions and the ability to derive maximum satisfaction from a given utility, or between the development of new tastes and less fatigue and more leisure time. On the quantitative side of his 'needs' theory of distribution, there was a necessary relation between reward and productivity, which could also have a qualitative impact on the connection between incentives and the production of good quality goods and services. Again, quantitatively, there was a necessary correspondence, according to his underconsumptionist theory, between income distribution and therefore consumption, on the one hand, and production, on the other.

Moreover, in organic terms, increased leisure would provide time for the mass of the population to develop the 'arts' of production, as well as the 'arts' of consumption. This creative dimension was central to Hobson's reforming project. It was the product of what could be called an 'expressivist economy'. It was inspired by Ruskin's aesthetic vision, and entailed the qualitative impovement of both the consumptive and productive 'arts', so that work became more self-expressive, and less costly in human, subjective terms. And the objects of consumption would possess greater utility, because they would possess greater quality. Thus, within the framework of his 'New Utilitarianism', human costs would be minimised and utility maximised.[58] Ultimately, then, he wanted the equality of opportunity for all in this substantive, self-developmental sense, enshrined in both liberal and socialist theory. The possibilities of universal 'individuation' were, nevertheless, dependent upon the amount of objective wealth in society, and the degree to which the production of goods that satisfied routine needs had been mechanised and socialised.[59] Here, the state had a key part to play.

Redistributing the surplus: state instruments and agencies

Although Hobson saw trade unions as important agencies for realising his distributive principles of minimising human costs and maximising human utilities, they had two fundamental drawbacks. Often they were not strong enough to combat the power of capital.[60] Secondly, they were instrinsically sectionalist, having no natural claim on the economic surplus, which was a complex, collective product. It was made by many workers, who were not necessarily members of the union claiming an increased share of the surplus.[61] Thus, the state, because it represented the community as a whole, and had the power to control capital, had a central function in the redistributive process. Its objective was to reform the market. This was achieved in a variety of ways: first, by altering the stakes (taxation and socialisation of monopolies); secondly, by changing the rules of the game (wage boards and arbitration); thirdly, by modifying competition through strengthening the position of weaker contestants (equality of opportunity); and, lastly, by removing contestants from the game altogether (socialisation of monopolies).

Taxation played an important part in putting the 'unproductive' surplus into public hands, where it could be devoted to the 'progressive' collective consumption of society as a whole. Although he wanted taxes on inheritance,[62] he saw graduated income tax as the primary instrument in this redistributive process. He proposed that it should be levied on the principle of 'ability to bear', as defined by his notion of the 'unproductive' surplus, i.e. the remainder after the wear and tear and expenses of progress (i.e. needs defined in terms of increased productivity) had been paid for. To ascertain precisely the extent of the 'unproductive' surplus could only be achieved experimentally.[63]

Secondly, 'unproductive' surpluses, where they had accrued in monopolised industries under state control, or as a result of the state regulation of those industries, could be used to achieve all or any four of the following objectives: paying workers in these industries the 'high wages of efficiency', improving their working conditions, passing the surplus on to consumers through lower prices, or using them for general public expenditure.[64] And to ensure that all the population could achieve a minimum standard of consumption, he proposed that everyone should be paid a minimum wage regulated by Wage or Trade Boards and state arbitration.[65]

However, the main purpose of arbitration for Hobson was not merely to guarantee fair or minimum wages and conditions for their own sake. It was to reduce industrial conflict, which was itself an expression of the struggle over the distribution of the surplus.[66] Consistent with his view that all factors of production were entitled to rewards based upon 'needs', and that the state was the 'brain' and controller of society, which produced the surplus, he formulated a universal scheme of compulsory arbitration.[67] Because private, separatist struggles adversely affected other sections of the community, he wrote in the aftermath of the 1926 General Strike:

> the absolute right to lock-out or to strike must go. It is unjust, in that it is an appeal to force in a matter of disputed right: it is inhuman, because of the misery it causes to the workers: it is wasteful of the resources of capital and labour: it is wicked because it stirs up hate: it is anti-social in that it denies and disrupts the solidarity of the community.[68]

However, he later qualified this argument, at least by implication. He contextualised his position, so that the right to take industrial action arose only when 'a genuinely democratic rule embraces the economic system, and when public service and not personal profit is the regulative principle'.[69]

Reducing the costs of production: state instruments and agencies

On the production side, the state could intervene to make the creation of the surplus less costly and more efficient in human terms. First, he wanted the state to foster conditions in which the distribution of labour would ensure, for example, that women and children did not have to perform hard, and arduous physical tasks.[70]

The state could also regulate employment contracts to protect workers from becoming victims of their own weakness, ignorance or carelessness. He additionally suggested legislation on employers' liability, and health and safety at work.[71] Further, he proposed that state wage and arbitration boards could be employed to make encroachments into the 'surplus', in order to improve the hours and conditions of work.[72] Finally, he wanted state-organised insurance as protection against injury or loss of livelihood.[73]

More significantly, human costs could be dramatically reduced by legislation shortening the working day, to at least eight hours. This would greatly alleviate physical and mental fatigue.[74] Moreover, shorter working hours would enable workers to derive greater utility from a given body of wealth.[75] Above all, they would mitigate some of the worst effects of the division of labour by enabling workers to develop their all-round potentials, through greater 'individuation' outside the workplace. Indeed, Hobson called increased leisure 'the opportunity of opportunities' – 'the condition of all effective social reconstruction and progress'.[76] Increased leisure was crucial to individual education, creativity, 'play' and invention.[77] Equally important, it was vital to social and political life. It enabled greater participation in voluntary social organisations and in political activities.[78]

Implementing equality of economic opportunity

Hobson also justified state intervention on the ground that it realised the principle of equal economic opportunity. He put great stress on this argument before the the First World War, when seeking to win over fellow Liberals to his position. Although he used the argument less after the war, it remained a central aspect of his reform programme.[79] If various markets were reformed through the application of this principle, 'unearned' surpluses gained through scarcity, especially excessive rents of ability, would be eliminated.[80]

Precisely what forms of intervention he had in mind to increase equality of opportunity were most clearly displayed in *The Crisis of Liberalism*.[81] They consisted of: (1) equal access to land, either

91

through public ownership or taxation of land values; (2) in order to ensure liberty to develop practical faculties and mobility of labour, the railways had to be nationalised, so that cheap rates and frequent services could be introduced; (3) equal access to sources of power, especially electricity – as a private monopoly it encroached upon the 'liberty of trade'; (4) equal access to capital through state-organised credit; (5) state insurance against unforeseen economic and health contingencies, in order to make full use of these opportunities; (6) equal access to law, which should become a public, rather than a private profession – private litigants should be relieved of all legal expenses; (7) equality of access to knowledge and culture – this was the 'opportunity of opportunities'.[82] The state should extend free general and technical education, and build more free libraries. In addition, there should also be cheap literature. Hobson, in the *Industrial System,* also interpreted various reforms as increasing equality of opportunity through enhancing the bargaining strength of workers *vis-à-vis* relation to capital. For example:

> Land reform will help to relieve congestion of the labour market; unemployed relief and old age pensions will economise the financial resources of the workers and their unions; education, poor law reforms, the repression of sweating conditions, will help to build up a more solid basis of working class organisation.[83]

State ownership and control: striking the balance

Although he appealed to the liberal principle of equality of opportunity in his proposals for nationalisation, he constantly sought to reassure liberals of two things: that clear limits to this process could be established; and that the enlargement of state bureaucracy, consequent upon the socialisation of certain sections of industry, need not be an unmitigated evil.

In his demarcation of the public and private boundaries of state ownership, we have the clearest example of Hobson attempting to bring about a peaceful and fruitful coexistence between liberal and socialist, individualist and collectivist principles. Although he developed his own rationale for a mixed economy, he was to some extent following in the footsteps of his friend William Clarke.[84]

His overall thesis was fairly straightforward.[85] He made a fundamental distinction between routine wants, common to all individuals, and more individualised ones, although both were subject to evolutionary change.[86] The former were increasingly met by goods produced by machine; the latter by 'art'.[87] Machine production tended to become monopolised and wasteful, in a double sense: first, because it accrued unproductive surpluses; and, secondly, through wasteful competition and trade fluctuations that resulted from this surplus.[88] These monopolies, along with natural monopolies were therefore ripe for state control, or ownership. [89] The cardinal rationale for such socialisation was that it would create the basis for greater individuation:

> As the elements of steady common consumption grow in number, the common organisation of activity to supply them will grow and where the supply has at first been left to private enterprise, the abuse of power and growing inconveniences of competition will drive them into public industry. But since the very *raison d'être* of this increased social co-hesiveness is to economise and enrich the individual life, and to enable the play of individual energy to assume higher forms out of which more individual satisfaction may accrue, and more human effort will take shape in industries which will be left to individual initiative and control, the arts in which the freedom of personal spontaneity will find scope in the expression of physical or moral beauty and fitness and the attainment of intellectual truth ...[90]

Thus routine, physical wants would be satisfied by efficient socialised machine production, which, in turn, would create the necessary conditions, especially through increased leisure, for individuated production and consumption. More time would be devoted to the cultivation of individual wants, as aesthetic, moral and intellectual potentials became increasingly realised.[91] These needs, machine production could not satisfy. Only individualised production would do, production that involved skill and creativity, with few attendant human costs, in contrast to machine production.[92] Thus, in evolutionary terms, socialised production formed the basis for the transition from 'quantitative' production to individuated, 'qualitative' production. Hence, outside the area of the satisfaction of routine needs, the market and private ownership of the means of production would reign supreme. Indeed, Hobson designated this sphere as the mainspring of industrial progress: 'Over a large area of industry, prize-money, in the shape of profit, must continue to be a serviceable method of getting the best results of inventive ability, risk, and enterprise, into the productivity of industry.' He argued that the sense of public service could not effectively operate upon 'all types of mind so as to get the best they have to give in contributions towards technological and business ability...'.[93] However, he did hope, although not with great conviction, that the worst effects of selfishness could be modified by encouraging a sense of social service through education.[94]

We should note that the boundaries between private and socialised industries were not immovable. These could change when certain products that originally catered for individual tastes became mechanically provided, routine wants for the mass of the population. However, his own, immediate and most important proposals consisted of the socialisation of those routine industries and services which had become monopolised, such as money, transport, power, iron and steel.[95] In addition, he called for the state control of standardised goods that were imported and exported. He also recognised that standardisation and individuation applied to different stages of the production process, for example, clothes, furniture and recreation; the earlier stages being standardised, the latter individuated.[96] Whether or not industries and resources should come under state control depended not merely on the nature of consumption but also on the type of materials used in, or conditions of, production, i.e. whether they were identical. They were clearly not in the case of agriculture, and here he still allowed some scope for private initiative.[97.]

Bureaucracy and democracy

Hobson wished to assuage two major liberal fears associated with state-run industry: that a loss of incentive and enterprise would occur, precipitating a reduction of output; and that such industry would be controlled by a bureaucracy, unresponsive both to rank-and-file employees and the public.

On the question of efficiency and innovation, Hobson had a number of answers. At one level, he could accept that little innovation would occur, but that this would be counterbalanced by benefits elsewhere. As we have already seen, he hoped that the socialisation of routine industries, by reducing waste and productively distributing the surplus, would allow for greater individuation of consumption and production in the private sphere.[98] Moreover, he even contemplated the possibility of the production of less objective wealth, on condition that this was offset by reduced human cost.[99] Yet, he normally assumed that production and innovation need not necessarily be adversely affected. Public industry did not have to face the wastes of private competition, and it could benefit from the economies of scale.[100] Further, innovation could continue, either because experience demonstrated that greed was not the key incentive to invention or, if it was, then material (or ego-boosting) rewards could still be used.[101] Somewhat later he argued that in some instances where innovation was crucial, as in railways, banking, coal mining and electricity supply, a 'half-way' house of private administration and public control could be established.[102]

As for the problem of bureaucracy, he contended that the superior bureaucratic mind had to be eliminated by: first, improving education, so that the 'poorer classes' could enter all echelons of public service; secondly, by reducing differentials in pay and conditions; thirdly, by opening up these public departments to criticism; fourthly, by recognising trade unionism in public service; and, finally, by allowing public employees the right of appeal to an independent public authority against arbitrary management.[103] After the First World War Hobson, probably as a result of his reflections upon state incursions into individual liberty during the war, put greater stress on the democratisation of the state and public industries as the antidote to bureaucracy (although, as we shall see in the next section, there were other reasons for wanting greater democratisation). He called for the establishment of organisational networks, representing producers and consumers.[104] Yet Hobson believed that ultimately the problem of bureaucracy could not be 'overcome by the most carefully-balanced series of constitutional checks'. Rather, the solution depended upon 'the intelligence and goodwill which the private citizens bring upon the public life, and upon the existence of corresponding qualities and sentiments in the public servants'.[105]

The insufficiency of economic reform

At this stage, we ought to note that the scope of Hobson's reforms was not confined solely to putting the unproductive surplus to productive use. His focus was much wider. First, the reform of international political and economic relations was vital because they impinged upon domestic social progress. Secondly, his desire for qualitative human improvement led him to advocate eugenic reform. Thirdly, he held political reform as signally important, not only as a means to dissipate the unproductive surplus and to control bureaucracy. He also valued it for its instrinsic effects. It fostered citizenship. Indeed, his interest in economic reform arose from his overriding concern to create a just and harmonious society, where sectional conflict was absent, and citizens worked for the common good, while simultaneously realising their individual potentials.

Democratic reform

Hobson's demand for greater democracy was in keeping with the traditional liberal opposition to 'class' government. It was central in overcoming the resistance of vested interests, the forces of 'improperty', that stood in the way of 'progress'.[106] For example, due to the absence of democracy, foreign policy was under plutocratic control. This led to the marginalisation of social issues, because vested interests could always generate international tensions, which then took precedence on the political agenda.[107] During and after the First World War Hobson wanted single-issue campaigners to realise that their efforts would be undermined by vested interests, unless they subsumed their concerns within a broader movement which sought to extend democracy.[108] Equally important, he saw democracy as integral to the development of sound public judgement: by involving citizens in political deliberation, they would become less 'mob-minded'.[109] Moreover, democratic reform, especially of the industrial structure, was essential in fostering a 'general will' in economic affairs, generating a form of consciousness that transcended workers' sectionalism.[110]

As for specific proposals, apart from those concerning the control of foreign policy[111] and industrial democracy, they were aimed at restricting the power of the Cabinet, by bringing it more firmly under the control of the majority party in Parliament.[112] Before the First World War he made other proposals, such as the abolition of the House of Lords veto, shorter parliaments, an extension of the franchise, presumably to include women, and 'adequate reforms of the electoral machinery'.[113] He also wanted refendums to be used,[114] although later he became less enthusiastic about this measure.[115]

However, Hobson argued that these reforms had to be buttressed by greater economic equality in order to be fully effective. Although he did not clearly indicate what he meant, he could have been referring to the fact that without such equality, vested interests could and would always pervert the popular will, and individuals would not have the time to participate in public life. Of equal importance, democratic structures would only work properly if there was generated a 'growth of public intelligence and conscience' making the 'general will' a reality. (116) Here, educational reform was vital. The content of education required alteration, in order to prepare people for citizenship (117) Hobson envisaged a type of school instruction that was less patriotic and militaristic, and in which religious bias was absent. Higher education, he proposed, should be less narrowly utilitarian and more broadly cultural.(118)

Eugenics

For Hobson, social progress would not be complete without society addressing itself to the 'population question'. Throughout his political and intellectual career, he shared the same concern as the Social Darwinists. The combatting of 'racial' degeneration was imperative. The problem assumed a greater urgency during the Boer War, when army recruitment revealed the extent of the 'unfitness' of the British population. However, he contended that the Social Darwinist survival-of-the fittest argument was doubly flawed. It failed to take into account that, as a result of human evolution, the mode of competition was changing from struggles over physical survival, with its wastefulness, to forms of cerebral combat, which advanced human culture.[119] Further, it begged the question as to what was the most desirable type of human being that ought to be produced.[120]

Hobson took it for granted that the kind of person to be 'cultivated' should not only be physically healthy but also mentally 'fit', in possession of well-developed intellectual, moral and aesthetic abilities. His proposals for human stirpiculture changed over the years. At first he adopted a hard-line interventionist stance. In *The Social Problem,* he wanted to outlaw the 'unfit' from reproducing,[121] whilst in *Work and Wealth,* he believed that the problem would spontaneously disappear as living standards improved.[122] After the First World War he suggested that the state should encourage good 'stock', by improving living standards of the population through family and tax allowances, insurance benefits, expenditure on public health and housing, improved public education, wider dissemination of knowledge of heredity and birth control, and by introducing immigration laws.[123] He also proposed state support for the children of the highly gifted.[124]

Conclusion

Whilst the dissipation of the 'unproductive' surplus was not the sole object of reform, it nevertheless remained his central one. Hobson's evolutionary, organic perspective told him that for the first time in human history the possibility of universal self-realisation existed. Machine production created huge surpluses, beyond those required for immediate physical survival. These surpluses could be used for good or ill. Universalising the benefits of the machine necessitated the extension of the state, which was central to attaining his 'New Utilitarian' objectives. These were 'new' in the sense that, following Mill, he brought qualitative satisfaction within the sweep of the felicific calculus.

Indeed, this combination of the 'quantitative' and the 'qualitative' was at the heart of his attempt to reconcile liberal and socialist principles. For him, the interdependence between quantitative and qualitative needs reflected human similarities, as well as existing and potential differences. This provided the foundation of his liberal-socialist synthesis. Pure liberalism failed to take into account the extent to which human beings had common, quantitative, needs; pure socialism did not fully appreciate human individuality, expressed in 'qualitative' needs. The state's economic boundaries were clear. It should only be concerned with ministering to quantitative needs, which people had in common. Where human needs, capacities and aspirations were different, its jurisdiction should end. Yet people could realise their individuality precisely because the state attended to their common needs.

Thus, the state, through the regulation of the production and distribution of goods satisfying common 'routine' wants and increasing the amount of leisure time, laid the basis for what might be called an 'expressivist economy' of individuated production and consumption, a vision inspired by John Ruskin. Indeed, Hobson's central intellectual task can be seen as the translation of the Ruskinian vision into a form appropriate to the conditions created by modern industrialism. It entailed the establishment of a framework in which the 'arts' of production and consumption could freely flourish. Paradoxically, the overriding purpose of Hobson's economic reform was to end the tyranny of 'economics' in people's lives, to transform it from the precipitating factor of human misery to the predisposing factor of human fulfilment.[125] This was the ultimate meaning that he attached to Ruskin's maxim, 'There is no wealth but life.'

5 Imperialism

Hobson's writings on international affairs, especially imperialism, were integral to his overall project of modernising liberal theory.[1] His seminal work, *Imperialism: A Study*, to which all his subsequent writings on international matters were effectively an extended footnote, was written against the background of the Boer War (1899–1902). The war wrought havoc within the ranks of the Liberal Party. It brought the differences between the imperialists and the 'Little Englanders' to a climax. Hobson believed that the party was on the verge of collapse, especially after its catastrophic showing in the so-called 'Khaki' elections in October 1900. In 1901 he joined the widespread debate on the left, both inside and outside the Party, on the question of political realignment. He publicly explored the possibility of bringing a new party into being, based upon a platform of anti-imperialism and social reform, and consisting of trade unionists, moderate socialists and middle-class progressives, such as himself. *Imperialism* sought to show that anti-imperialists and social reformers of whatever class or 'fad' had a common cause in the abolition of the 'unproductive' surplus that was ultimately responsible for the ills of poverty, unemployment, militarism and imperialism.

In advocating this remedy, he also wished to demonstrate to a wider public that the 'social' imperialist solution to Britain's economic and social problems was fallacious. Both the Liberal Unionists, under the leadership of Joseph Chamberlain, Colonial Secretary until 1903, and the Liberal Imperialists, headed by Lord Rosebery, who was Prime Minister between 1894 and 1895, in the wake of Gladstone's resignation, held that economic prosperity, social reform and imperialism were interdependent. Whilst the Liberal Imperialists and Chamberlainites differed over the question of free trade, or 'Tariff Reform' as it became known, both agreed that a strong and growing Empire was vital to Britain's economic future, and hence the capacity to finance social improvement. In turn, social reform by generating social cohesion and a healthy and educated population enhanced Britain's 'national' or 'social' efficiency, and therefore its ability to remain a major imperial power. *Imperialism* aimed to demonstrate that the social imperialist formula was undesirable and unworkable. This entailed, first, an attack on the ideological legitimation of imperialism and its practice; and, secondly, an analysis of its causes and cures. As with his writings on economic and social reform, he took into account new 'facts', especially the existence of large European empires with their attendant 'burdens', and new ideas that led him to either revise or embellish certain aspects of the liberal tradition. In condemning, explaining and remedying imperialism, he attempted to synthesise liberalism in its Cobdenite form with his organic perspective and theory of underconsumption. In addition, he borrowed freely from contemporary writings on social psychology and anthropology.

Condemning imperialism

Despite his reputation as an anti-imperialist, Hobson did not condemn all forms of imperialism. Thus, he distinguished between 'sane'[2] and 'legitimate'[3] imperialism on the one hand, and 'insane'[4] and 'aggressive'[5] imperialism, on the other. The types of imperialism that Hobson singled out for hostile treatment were manifestations of what he called the 'New Imperialism', a global phenomenon that started approximately in 1870. He characterised the New Imperialism as consisting of: (1) competing empires, rather than all-embracing single empires of the past;[6] (2) the dominance of financial or investment capital over mercantile interests;[7] and (3) the absorption of new territories populated by culturally unassimilable peoples for whom self-government was not intended by the imperial powers.[8] This contrasted sharply with the previous colonialism, which he regarded as legitimate because it constituted a 'natural outflow of nationality' to sparsely populated areas and was marked by the evolution of self-governing insitutions.[9]

Along with many other so-called 'Little Englanders' who opposed the Boer War, Hobson relied heavily on Cobden's arguments which concentrated upon the impact of imperialism upon the imperialist powers themselves.[10] Hobson followed Cobden closely in this 'imperialism does not pay' formulation:

> the new Imperialism ... consumes to an illimitable extent the financial resources of a nation by military preparation ... burdening posterity with heavy loads of debt. Absorbing the public money, time, interest and energy on costly and unprofitable work of territorial aggrandisement, it thus wastes those energies of public life in the governing classes and the nations which are needed for internal reforms and for the cultivation of the arts of material and intellectual progress at home. Finally, the spirit, the policy and the methods of imperialism are hostile to the institutions of popular self-government, favouring forms of political tyranny and social authority which are the deadly enemies of effective liberty and equality.[11]

Hobson elaborated upon the last point by demonstrating the incompatibility of imperialism and democracy in Britain. The growth of the military was harmful to democratic citizenship. Good soldiers did not make good citizens, because they were not encouraged to develop moral sensibilities and socially responsible attitudes.[12] The Empire also spawned a new stratum of colonial administrators imbued with an autocratic spirit, adding to the weight of reaction when they returned from the imperial outposts.[13] Indeed, the 'burdens' of Empire and the international conflicts engendered by imperial questions had produced a large and highly centralised bureaucracy which, along with the Cabinet, was not subject to proper parliamentary control. This loss of parliamentary efficacy was matched by a decline in the party system. It had previously flourished on the basis of party divisions arising from differences on domestic issues. Because imperial problems now predominated on the parliamentary agenda, such conflicts were supplanted by an unhealthy consensus.[14]

Hobson also echoed Cobden in stressing the costs of colonisation. And moving away from an earlier protectionist position,[15] he upeld the principle of free trade, arguing, in opposition to the imperialists, that trade did not follow the flag.[16] Yet, in keeping with his underconsumptionism, he departed from the spirit of free trade. He asserted that foreign trade was diminishing in relation to Britain's total industrial activity and that dependence on it could be reduced further if income were more equitably distributed.[17]

He added one final Cobdenite cost to the debit side of the ledger: the possibility of retribution. His case, though, was not in the theological terms of Cobden but of biology, derived from his organic perspective. Imperialism was akin to parasitism, and parasites inevitably decayed in nature.[18] Indeed, this argument was merely echoing an 'organically' modified version of Ruskin's biblically derived remonstration against parasitism: 'Whosoever will not work, neither *can* he eat.'[19]

Hobson borrowed one further crucial argument from Ruskin in condemning imperialism. Drawing a qualitative inference from Ruskin's saying 'There is no wealth but life', he attacked the modern obsession with quantitative, as opposed to qualitative, values, as expressed not only in economic theory but also as implicit in the justification of imperialism.

He not only focused upon the effects of imperialism for the imperialist nations. He vehemently criticised the way in which these nations treated the 'lower races' of Africa and the sub-tropics.

He passionately denounced the imperialist claim to be civilizing these races. It was blatant hypocrisy.[20] What occurred in reality was 'insane' imperialism, 'which hands over the races to the exploitation of white colonists who will use them as "live tools" and their lands as repositories of mining or other profitable treasure'.[21] He documented a large number of imperialist practices which drove these races from their lands and forced them to work for the white man.[22] The argument that the West was civilizing the populations of India and China was even more specious. These peoples possessed cultures that were just as sophisticated as those of the West. They merely happened to be different.[23] Furthermore, the British in India had destroyed indigenous industries and local self-government. And he contemplated the collapse of Chinese culture and character as a result of Western economic and political incursions.[24]

Explaining imperialism

Hobson, in getting to grips with the origins of the New Imperialism, partly relied on Cobdenite explanation – the conspiracy theory of 'sinister interests'. Cobden had singled out the landed aristocracy and the suppliers to the armed forces as the beneficiaries and, *therefore*, as the proponents of aggressive international posturing. This *cui bono* explanation figured prominently in *Imperialism*.[25] But Hobson, in the light of his interpretation of the Boer War, which he saw as caused by finance capitalists, and as a result of his observation that modern capitalism was evolving towards monopoly, changed the central dramatis personae: plutocrats were substituted for aristocrats, who were left with the occasional walk-on part.[26]

He combined this explanation with his more famous account of the genesis of modern imperialism, underconsumptionism, which he regarded as the 'economic taproot'. Lack of domestic demand for current production created surplus capital that sought outlets abroad. Two comments can be made about Hobson's hypothesis. First, he did not originate the surplus capital theory of imperialism. Businessmen in the 1890s employed it to *justify* imperialism.[27] His originality lay rather in his account for this glut of capital. Secondly, his underconsumptionist explanation was somewhat detached from his conspiracy theory in *Imperialism*, probably due to the fact that this work consisted of a compilation of loosely connected magazine articles. These two explanations were eventually synthesised in the 1906 revised edition of *The Evolution of Modern Capitalism* .[28]

One important question that Hobson had to confront as a consequence of his conspiracy theory was that, if so few people actually benefited from imperialism, why did it find favour with wide sections of the British population when it was so palpably irrational and against their interests? He explained it as a form of 'social pathology'.[29] In *The Psychology of Jingoism* and *Imperialism* he relied heavily, if not uncritically, on Le Bon's *The Crowd*, and he may have gained further insights from his friends William Clarke and Graham Wallas. He saw the 'mob mind' of jingoism as the product of certain trends in urban industrial civilization. Mechanical and uniform work operations, overcrowding, and superficial and homogeneous leisure pursuits destroyed the capacity for independent rational thought amongst the masses.[30] The music hall, and particularly the 'yellow press', much of which was controlled by finance capitalists, stirred up atavistic lusts, which, whilst necessary for physical survival· in the past, were now redundant in evolutionary terms. The growth of passive spectator sports reinforced this process.[31]

This outburst of irrationality entailed the debasement of thought and language. Hobson was strikingly modern in the way in which he analysed imperialist 'ideology'. Although he did not use the term in *Imperialism*, it has now become the common coin of intellectual exchange. He postulated that the connection between self-interest and the justification of imperialism was obscure even to the beneficiaries themselves, apart from the finance capitalists. The ideological defence of imperialism was the result of self-deception.[32] People blinded themselves as to what was really happening to the subject races, as a consequence of Britain's imperial domination, through inconsistent thinking and 'masked words' (Ruskin's phrase). These races were not ruled as a 'trust for civilisation'. White colonists in reality used them as 'live tools', and irresponsibly extracted natural resources from their lands.[33] Hobson also observed how the 'educated classes' had become imbued with imperialist ideology: 'the church, the press, the schools and colleges, the political machine, the four chief instruments of popular education are accommodated to [imperialism's] service'.[34]

Remedying imperialism

Hobson's alternative to imperialism, in the long term, was a world polity of independent, democratic self-governing states, based upon free trade, international arbitration and minimal intergovernmental relations, a model strongly advocated by Cobden. In political terms 'genuine democracy' was the key solution to imperialism, by taking the control of foreign policy out of the hands of vested interests and making it accountable to the people, whose real interests lay in peaceful relations with other peoples.[35] Economically, the remedy was to destroy the 'taproot' of imperialism, by allowing higher wages and social reform to consume the 'unproductive' surplus. This would expand the domestic market, and reduce the need for foreign outlets for commodities and capital.[36]

These socio-economic reforms were justified by Hobson not only in narrow economic terms but also within his wider, organic evolutionary theory that he used to attack the Social Darwinist defence of imperialism. Such reforms, as an act of 'intensive' as opposed to 'extensive' cultivation, would be an expression of human moral and intellectual development. They would demonstrate that international competition had progressed from the physical survival of the fittest to cultural conflict, the true test of 'social efficiency'. Thus, in proferring his own brand of evolutionary positivism he stated:

> Biology demands as a condition of world-progress that the struggle of nations or races continue; but as the world grows more rational it will in similar fashion rationalise the rules of that ring, imposing a fairer test of forms of national fitness.[37]

He not only accepted the fundamental Social Darwinian belief in the virtue of competition, he also endorsed the need to create better human 'stock'. To achieve this he advocated eugenics, which he suggested should be applied on an international scale.[38]

Hobson's organic theory also featured in his justification of the reform of relations between the imperialist states and the 'lower races', who were not immediately destined for self-government. In rejecting the Cobdenite solution of separation, he proposed a form of trusteeship – his 'sane' or 'legitimate' imperialism – by an 'organised representation of civilised humanity', a kind of international welfare state. This scheme prefigured the mandate system of the League of Nations. In support of this form of intervention, he maintained that just as the organic analogy could be used to stress individual interdependence within a collective whole in opposition to *laissez-faire* within the domestic realm, so too on an international scale: 'There can no more be absolute nationalism in the society of nations than absolute individualism in the single nation.' (39) He agreed with much of the imperialist case as advanced by the Fabians, Kidd and Giddings: 'civilised humanity' could legitimately intervene in the tropics and sub-tropics where the 'lower races' were not developing their resources required by the 'European races'.[40]

Persuading indigenous populations to perform wage labour should, however not be by compulsion but through 'legitimate induce-ments', namely 'the growth of population with increased difficulty in getting a full easy subsistence from the soil' and 'the pressure of new needs and a rising standard of consumption'.[41] He advanced three further arguments in favour of intervention. The 'lower races' needed protection from the hordes of 'private adventurers, slavers, piratical traders, treasure hunters, [and] concession mongers'.[42] And, secondly, without some form of organised international intervention, these populations would be open to manipulation by 'native or imported rulers',who, 'playing upon the religious fanaticism or the combative instincts of great hordes of semi-savages, may impose upon them so effective a military discipline as to give terrible significance to some black or yellow "peril".'[43] Thirdly, he justified this 'sane' imperialism on the grounds of cultural superiority, reminiscent of Mill's position, already noted in Chapter 1. It would enhance the 'self-development' of the 'low-typed unprogressive races'. In uncompromising terms, Hobson contended that:

> there can be no inherent natural right in a people to refuse that measure of compulsory education which shall raise it from childhood to manhood in the order of nationalities. The analogy furnished by the education of a child is prima facie a sound one, and is not invalidated by the dangerous abuses to which it is exposed in practice.[44]

He did, though, reject any idea that India and China should be administered by an 'organised representation of civilised human-ity'. Here he invoked, in a rather selective fashion, the principle of cultural relativism. He challenged the assumption that civilisa-tions 'are at root one and the same, that they have a common nature and a common soil'.[45] Earlier he had argued, probably in the light of the anthropological works of Mary Kingsley, that 'if civilisation is multi-form, we cannot say that one civilisation is better than another, only that it is different'.[46] Thus, Hobson, in suggesting that the West had no business interfering in these Eastern civilisations, by implication followed Cobden's policy of separatism that he had advocated especially for India.

During the First World War Hobson attached even greater significance to the establishment of an 'organised representation of civilised humanity'. Under the aegis of an international government, it would help create international conditions for a greater equality of economic opportunity, thereby helping to undermine the forces of imperialism and protectionism within the advanced capitalist powers. Areas administered by this body would be subject to an 'open door' policy, allowing investment and trade on equal terms from all countries.[47]

Of equal significance, the war induced Hobson to work out a plan for international arbitration, already suggested in *Imperialism*, building it into a system of international government. The premises justifying this system paralleled Hobson's *étatisme* at the domestic level. Just as antagonisms stemming from the defects of capitalism could be overcome by state action, overriding the sovereignty of the individual, so at the international level. He proposed a supranational body that overrode national sovereignty, and was able to enforce collective rules and decisions. In particular, states that refused to accept either the arbitration decisions or concilation proposals made by this body would be compelled to do so by military or economic sanctions.[48]

After imperialism

Although *Imperialism* has correctly come to be regarded as one of the classic commentaries on modern international politics, Hobson came to appreciate that he had left a number of theoretical tensions and problems unattended. They arose principally from his underconsumptionist analysis and his Cobdenism, both in its 'pure' and modified form (namely his portrayal of the plutocracy rather than the aristocracy as imperialism's sinister interest-in-chief).

The first problem that underconsumptionism created was a vulnerability to the charge of economic determinism. In fact, he was aware of this danger both before and after *Imperialism*. At the time of the Boer War he acknowledged the case 'of Capitalism issuing Imperialism is of necessity imperfect. No play of historical forces is so simple as this'. [49] In his autobiography he wrote in self-criticism that *Imperialism* contained 'an excessive and too simple advocacy of the economic determination of history.'[50] Critics such as Norman Angell insisted that psychological factors had greater explanatory potency.[51] Yet, although he came to make concessions on this score, Hobson held fast to the primacy of economics, which determined the 'concrete application' of power politics, or was in the final analysis the 'dominant directive motive.'[52] He was probably referring here to the machinations of the financial magnates. However, Hobson, by insisting on the overriding importance of economic explanation, was not advancing a *deterministic* theory in any strict mechanical sense. Although underconsumption created the *conditions* for imperialism, the finance capitalists were the human agents, or precipitating factors, in this process.

Nevertheless, real difficulties stemmed from Hobson's attempt to integrate in various ways underconsumptionism with his reconstituted Cobdenite conspiracy theory and belief in the virtues of international trade and finance. First, his underconsumptionist, 'taproot' account of imperialism, and its concomitant redistributive solution, led Hobson in the first edition of *Imperialism* to suggest that Britain could, and ought, to become virtually self-sufficient,[53] Such a prescription has led Peter Cain, to identify what amounts to a hiatus in his thought. Between 1898 and 1902 Hobson apparently thought that 'foreign trade and investment as a whole was largely ... unnecessary', and he had 'a very unfavourable analysis of the process of international exchange, an analysis which is very different indeed from the fulsome tributes of 1906-11'.[54] What occurred, however, was more a change of emphasis than position. True, in *Imperialism* he followed the logic of his underconsumptionism in his semi-autarkic recommendations. Yet, in this work as a Cobdenite, he consistently stressed the great benefits of the internationalisation of the world economy. Thus, finance capital was crucial to world economic development. This view was revealed, by implication, in his endorsement of 'sane' imperialism. He stated: 'It is the great practical business of the country to explore and develop, by every method which science can devise, the hidden natural and human resources of the globe.'[55] Such an objective would necessitate foreign investment. Thus, although in *An Economic Interpretation of Investment* he was eulogistic about foreign investment: 'finance capital provided through joint stock companies is now the great fertilising stream in world industry', [56] this indicates not a change of view, but the continuation of tension that can be detected in *Imperialism*. This stemmed from the colliding paradigms of underconsumptionism and Cobdenism.

This tension manifested itself in another way, which again demonstrates that he did not have a 'very unfavourable analysis of the process of international exchange' in *Imperialism*. In true Cobdenite vein, he argued that international finance was a force for world peace. Anticipating Karl Kautsky's notorious theory of 'ultra-imperialism'[57] he asserted: 'the rapid growth of effective internationalism in the financial and great industrial magnates, who seem destined more and more to control national politics, may in the near future render such [imperialist] wars impossible'.[58] He repeated the claim more rhapsodically in a *An Economic Interpretation of Investment*:' modern finance is the great sympathetic system in an economic organism in which political divisions are of constantly diminishing importance'.[59]

Yet paradoxically Hobson maintained in *Imperialism* that finance capital had inherently belligerent propensities. It was the 'governor of the imperial engine' and 'imperialism ... implies militarism now and ruinous wars in the future'. [60] He displayed a similar ambiguity in his attitude towards investors and those capitalists not involved in finance. Thus, he could, on the one hand, exonerate the rank-and-file investor from belligerent behaviour, but, on the other hand, he could see their interests lying in imperial expansion.[61] By the same token he sometimes accused manufacturers with fostering imperialism, while at others he viewed them as essentially non-imperialist.[62]

The pacific view of international trade and finance which he had inherited from Cobden that created this equivocation, disappeared as a result of his reflections on the Great War, whose advent he had considered a 'surprise'.[64]

> It is important that a fundamental assumption of Cobdenism, and of liberalism to which it appertained, that war and militarism were doomed to disappear with the advance of industry and commerce, is definitely false. Indeed, a large part of the analysis upon which we are engaged is devoted to showing how modern capitalism, both in its structure and its operations, requires, feeds and utilises militarism.[64]

Henceforth, he stressed the systemic explanation, associated with his underconsumptionism. This implied that an unreformed capitalism was inherently antagonistic on an international scale.[65] So for example, by 1938 he had clarified his attitude towards manufacturers in a way that was consistent with underconsumptionism. Exporters of goods were much more strongly featured as a force for imperialism, in contrast to his original position.[66]

Hobson's attempt to mix underconsumptionism with Cobdenism yielded one final problem, spotted by his friend and collaborator on the *Nation* H. N. Brailsford. He observed that Hobson had argued that imperialism could not be eliminated until 'the axe is laid at the economic root of the tree', and yet had simultaneously endeavoured to lay down the foundation of international government.[67] The first solution was implicit in his underconsumptionist analysis, and assumed that politics was a function of monopoly capitalism; his second, political one, derived from his Cobdenism, assumed that political superstructures could be detached from capitalism. He did, though, come to recognise that a tension existed between these two remedies. In the 1930s he avoided having to choose between them, by recommending a policy of 'wise opportunism'.[68] By 1938, however, possibly in the light of the League of Nations' failure to prevent the drift towards global confrontation, he abandoned this position, and emphasised domestic (i.e. economic) reform as a precondition for world peace.

> The great lesson of the War and the even more important lesson of the Peace thus brought home to me the truth that justice as well as charity begins at home. It is impracticable to hope for international peace and justice in international affairs unless the conditions for internal peace and justice within the nations have already been substantially obtained.[69]

Hobson then finally chose to prioritise domestic reform in resolving international conflict. A symmetry thus emerged between this strategy for international reform and his underconsumptionist explanation of imperialism.

Thus, over time, as his Cobdenite faith in the pacific tendencies of capitalism waned, his explanation of, and his related solutions to, imperialism became more internally coherent. This is not to suggest that his overall perspective on imperialism, especially in an unmodified form, cannot be subject to criticism. For example, his explanation of imperialism in terms of underconsumptionism and capitalist conspiracy as a universal hypothesis, in accounting for all forms of late nineteenth-century and twentieth-century imperialism, has obvious weaknesses. It assumes too readily that the state is transparently the agent of the monopoly capitalists, and that all imperialist states possessed large amounts of surplus capital that required a 'vent'.[70] Secondly, Hobson's justification of mandates, his 'sane' imperialism, can be regarded with scepticism. In claiming that the needs of European industry and consumer, and that the enhancement of global productivity, were paramount, he displayed a profound Eurocentrism and a rather narrow 'productivism'. Indeed, whether his organic analogy, which he used to endorse state intervention within the domestic realm. could be simply applied on an international scale is dubious. Domestically, the analogy could be used to justify interference with the rights of the wealthy, whose ownership of the 'unproductive' surplus diseased the body politic and 'economic'. This infringement of individual rights included income redistribution in order, *inter alia*, to increase economic opportunity for the majority of the population. Applied internationally, the analogy works out somewhat differently. It entailed interfering with the rights of peoples, permitting the unilateral extraction of resources by advanced, capitalist nations, and involved the imposition of wage labour on these populations.

In concluding, we should note that his 'sane' imperialism, which the organic analogy was invoked to defend, was no intellectual or political aberration on Hobson's part. It paralleled his hypothesis that the 'unproductive' surplus was *the* problem. A maladjusted capitalism was the problem, not capitalism as such. A properly regulated surplus was something from which all could derive an advantage. By the same token, at the international level, imperialists rather than imperialism were the problem. The proper regulation of overseas investment in areas inhabited by the 'lower races' through an 'open door' policy and a mandate system would yield universal benefits and avoid inter-imperial conflict. And, just as he sought a 'middle way' between capitalism and socialism in the domestic sphere, so in terms of foreign policy he tried to steer between imperialism and anti-imperialism. The issue was to persuade the imperialist powers to clean up their act. To put the point crudely: for the 'lower races' in the he wanted imperialism with a 'human face'.

6 Strategy and agency

Hobson's reform programme aimed to unite the desirable with the feasible. For him it made good ethical sense: it fused liberal and socialist principles; it took account of the homogeneity and heterogeneity of human needs, as well as the individualistic and associative aspects of human behaviour. Yet his programme had a clear practical intent. He formulated it in the 1890s when, as already indicated, liberalism's fortunes seemed at rock-bottom. The party, effectively leaderless after Gladstone's departure, was internally divided by competing interest and reforming groups, and was externally threatened by the development of working-class political organisations which could undermine working-class allegiance to the Liberal Party. The overall object of his programme, with the dissipation of the 'unearned' at its centre, was to foster unity at two connected levels: the political and the social. Politically, Hobson wanted to unite single issue reformers and encourage co-operation between the Liberal Party and labour organisations, especially the ILP after the 1895 elections. At the social level, he wished to unite, just as his friend H. D. Lloyd did in the United States, the progressive members of the middle class such as himself, with the more progressive sections of the working class, trade unionists and moderate socialists.

In fashionable, Gramscian parlance, his aim was to create a new, 'historic bloc', committed to expanding the economic and welfare functions of the state. From the 1890s onwards he attempted to bring this 'bloc' into being, whatevever the precise configurations of the political terrain. The reforms he proposed were designed not only to create a progressive coalition, they could not, in fact, be realised without such a coalition. Throughout his fifty-year involvement in politics he was constantly aware of the strength of the forces of reaction, and the feebleness and disunity of the progressive movement. Within that span, the periods in which a remotely progressive government was in office were as follows: 1906–14 (Liberal), 1924 (Labour) and 1929–31 (Labour), namely, less than twelve years in total. Even in these years of governmental power, he constantly believed that the forces of progress were extremely fragile, requiring unification and external assistance (the Liberals from the Labour Party 1906–14 and Labour from the Liberal Party 1924, and 1929–31.)

Class alliances

The bedrock of the various political alliances he advocated throughout his political career was a middle- and working-class coalition. The working class was essential, because it had the 'voting power', the electoral muscle. Yet he adamantly believed that the middle class was equally crucial. It had the 'brains'. It had the truly 'hegemonic' capacities of leadership. Along with various members of the upper classes, it was the vital catalyst of reform. So, for example, his experience of the membership of the London Ethical Society, despite his sharp criticisms of its moral individualism, led him to maintain that 'any wider reforms of working class character demanded a prior process of moral instruction for the upper and middle classes'.[1] He claimed, although he was by no means consistent in this matter,[2] that the 'most important achievement of "practical socialism" has been as much the fruit of social compunction among the well-to-do classes as the organised working class force.'[3] The significance he attached to moralising the middle class perhaps explains why he was for over forty years a lecturer at the South Place Ethical Society, whose members were drawn mainly from the 'business and professional classes'.[4]

The middle and upper classes were pivotal to this alliance for another reason. They had the power to block social reconstruction: 'History makes it clear that mere numbers, mere quantity of physical force or even electoral power, cannot prevail against superior knowledge, organisation, habit of command and the possession of all the dominating positions in the political and economic system'.[5] They had to be won over by persuasion. Equally vital, he held, if only by implication, that the middle class was central to the running of society.[6] He had little faith in the hegemonic capacities of workers *qua* workers. For example, in discussing trade unionists he averred: 'Neither by education, selection or viewpoint are they well-suited for this wide and varied work [of running society].'[7] And in the 1920s he had doubts about the ruling skills of the Labour leaders. He wrote privately in 1927: "I wish I could find enough intelligence in labour leadership to reassure one for the future.[8] Although he was unhappy about society being run by 'untrained democrats', he believed that individual members of the working class could, through education, acquire the requisite skills.

In seeking to win the middle class to the progressive cause, Hobson relied on a mixture of guilt and self-interest. He employed a variation of Joseph Chamberlain's famous doctrine of 'ransome'. After the First World War he argued that revolutionary class conflict could be avoided only through a more equitable distribution of wealth.[9] Yet, as already noted, such a distribution had to appreciate fully the need for middle-class incentive.[10] He also pressed moral weapons into service. It was necessary to awaken a '"sense of sin" in the souls of these enemies', to sap their 'intellectual and moral defences...'[11]

In this 'hegemonic' process, proletarian revolution had to be avoided at all costs: 'a formally successful revolutionary force would leave the workers' minds poisoned and disabled for performance of their task. Effective government in any branch of conduct requires the real consent, not merely of the triumphant majority, but of the defeated minority', because success would 'require that a substantial number of the "capitalist class" are won over by the appeal to justice and humanity and recognise the need for conscious economic government.'[12] Further, he doubted whether the working class had the potential force to make a revolution: 'There is little reason to believe that the organisation of working peoples is anywhere possessed of the force required for a successful proletarian revolution.'[13] Finally, to be revolutionary was just not 'English':

> Englishmen are not prepared to hate or destroy 'the bourgeoisie'. Their reason, their humour, and their humanity protect them against the violence of a creed and behaviour to which Russian communism has succumbed. To Continental revolutionists this often appears as a 'softness' of head and heart. And in a sense it is. But this 'softness' has some place in the 'common sense' which keeps us from extremes.[14]

Political alliances

Hobson's plans for social reconstruction entailed not merely the co-operation of the middle and working classes. The forging of a political movement that could bring this about required uniting reformers of whatever social backgound.[15] Just as significant: such a movement required some sort of fusion of, or co-operation, between, middle-class Liberals and members of socialist-labour organisations. The precise form that this coalition would take was determined by his analysis of political forces, particularly the will and the capacity of various political parties to implement his reform progamme. Thus, in the 1890s until the Liberal landslide of 1906 he advocated various forms of co-operation and fusion. He was uncertain as to whether the Liberal Party would either survive or change sufficiently to embrace his proposals for social reform, and whether the ILP had the potential to supplant the Liberals as the progressive actor on the political scene, as socialist parties had begun to do on the Continent. In the wake of the Liberal victory at the polls in 1906, he was more committed to persuading the party to adopt his reforms, although he saw the Labour Party in this period as an important ginger group. However, by 1914–16 he had lost faith in the Liberal Party's progressive potential. It proved incapable of defending what he regarded as the most traditional of liberal principles – the rule of law (in relation to the Curragh Mutiny). And as the First World War unfolded, as part of a coalition government, it colluded in the serious erosion of democratic rights, individual liberties and free trade. In Hobson's mind, an intimate connection existed between the upholding of traditional liberal principles and social reform. The more individual liberties and democratic rights were lost, the harder it was to organise opposition against vested interests hindering social reform. He left the party in 1916, and became loosely associated with the Labour Party, eventually joining it in 1924, the year in which it formed a minority government. He then attempted to persuade it to adopt his reforming principles. Yet, whatever the exact location of the political milieu within which he operated, his message was the same: social reconstruction would be achieved only by a broad progressive movement, consisting of a wide range of social reformers and involving co-operation between Liberal and socialist labour organisations.

His endeavours to construct alignments and promote forms of co-operation and win over, first, the Liberal Party and, later, the Labour Party to his reforming perspective can be divided into approximately three distinct phases: 1895–1906 , 1906–16 and from 1916 onwards.

Towards a progressive party (1895–1906)

The key question for Hobson, as the 1890s wore on, was whether the Liberal Party could survive both as an effective political force and as a progressive agency, or whether it would follow the fate of certain Continental liberal parties. Unable to embrace seriously collectivist principles, they were being superseded by working-class socialist parties. As a result of this uncertainty, he, along with his friend William Clarke, in the latter half of the 1890s were formally independent of the Liberal Party [16] and consistently called for the formation of a 'progressive party', although the activity, form and composition of such a party remained unclear.[17]

We have already noted, in Chapter one, that in the early 1890s he was highly critical of the Liberal Party – Gladstone's obsession with Ireland and indifference to social issues, which was, to a significant extent, reflected throughout the party; the domination of the local caucuses by the 'money-bags'; and its lack of clear, unifying principles of social reform. The party's disastrous showing at the 1895 elections confirmed his criticisms. His pessimism about its future was reinforced by its refusal to field a working-class candidate at the East Bradford by-election in 1896, and its inability to regain this seat, which it had lost in 1895. He saw the result as demonstrating the 'utter break up of the Liberal Party'.[18] Although earlier he had been doubtful about the ILP's potential as a 'hegemonic' party,[19] because of its intellectually impoverished leadership, he now began to see it as possibly replacing the Liberal Party: 'If the new leaders of the ILP, who are mostly drawn from the middle classes show they can formulate a programme with even some semblance of practicality, it seems not impossible that they will suck the force out of the Liberal Party, as their fellow Socialists have done in Germany and Belgium.'[20] Yet, at the same time he could contemplate the possibility of the Liberal Party having a future if it ceased to be a 'middle class political organisation' and became more working class oriented in its policies.[21]. Thus, whilst Hobson may have genuinely believed that the party's demise was probable, he also felt that it had a slender chance of surviving if its composition and policies changed. Indeed, he may have been publicly predicting the party's collapse in order to panic the Party into accepting collectivist principles.[22] Nevertheless, as the century drew to a close any glimmer of progressivist hope in the Liberal Party seemed to have evaporated. He strongly criticised the party for its seeming capitulation to imperialism, effectively undermining its sacred, free trade principles, as well as its pretensions as a party of domestic reform, since in Hobson's eyes an aggressive foreign policy effectively deflected social issues away from the political agenda.[23] Moreover, the Liberal Party could not claim to be a radical reforming party in any formal sense: it had 'never manifested any serious intention to give a radical interpretation to the phrase [equality of opportunity] which would satisfy the organic conception of society. By every measure of tentative reform it has spread disunion among its members, and its programmes, instead of being an orderly display of principles, are a dramatic exhibition of intellectual anarchy.'[24]

His waning confidence in the Liberty Party provides the backdrop to his attempt to unify social reformers of different pet fixations and ideological creeds around a minimum programme that entailed a broadening of the state's functions. This unifying enterprise was both reflected in, and the product of, his membership of the Rainbow Circle, whose members played an active part in bringing about the kind of shift that was evident in the 1906–14 Liberal reforms. The Circle aimed to provide 'a rational and comprehensive view of political and social progress ... which could be ultimately formulated in a programme of action, and a rallying point for social reformers'. In order to develop such a programme, the Circle felt that three key areas ought to be explored:

(1) the reasons why the old Philosophical Radicals and the Manchester School of Economics can no longer furnish a ground for action in the political sphere; (2) the transition from this school of thought to the so-called 'New Radicalism' or Collectivist politics of today; (3) the basis, ethical, economic and political, of the newer politics, together with the practical applications and influences arising therefrom in the actual problems before us at the present time.[25]

Not only did the Circle see itself as a 'think-tank', it had proselytising intentions. It produced *The Progressive Review* in the autumn of 1896, with William Clarke as editor, Hobson as his assistant and Ramsay MacDonald as secretary. The 'chief object' of the *Review*, according to Hobson, was to 'gather up the fragments of the Liberal Party, and endeavour to form for them what they lack so conspicuously just now, principles and policy'. [26] For Hobson, though, one of these 'fragments' consisted of 'Labour–Socialist' elements,[27] and, formally, editorial policy remained neutral between the Tory and Liberal parties, probably in deference to the ILP, and possibly as a result of Fabian influence. However, the *Review* collapsed after eighteen months as a result of the conflicts between Clarke and MacDonald, and between imperialists and 'Little Englanders', low circulation and Clarke's ill-health.[28] After the *Review*'s demise Hobson persisted in his attempt to bring about a 'union of progressive forces'. At its fourth session, which lasted from October 1898 to June 1899, the Rainbow Circle discussed, at Hobson's instigation, topics likely to compose the practical programme for a 'progressive party': 'The Drink Traffic, The Empire, The House of Lords, the Land, The Weak and Home Rule'.[29] He argued that the prospects for a progressive party were good, because 'the principles upon which such a party must be based are already in existence in the form of a widely-held intellectual affinity. What is a matter of fact places the leaders of the Radical, the Socialist and the Labour groups much nearer to each other than their followers imagine.'[30]

Hobson strove most energetically to construct a 'progressive party' during the period of the Boer War (1899–1902). Not only did he believe that the Liberal Party was finished as a result of the cleavages wrought by the war, and reflected in the poor results of the Khaki elections of October 1900. He was no longer convinced that the party could be won over to the progressive cause. It was too closely implicated in the Tories' imperialist project. He sought a new realignment around leaders of the labour movement, some of whom had been by far the most consistent opponents of the war. Many had joined the anti-war Liberals to form the South African Conciliation Committee, established in November 1899, which called for an immediate peace.[31] For Hobson there were only two positions that could be adopted in relation to the war: for or against. In his mind, the Liberal centre grouping in Parliament was almost as much at fault as the Liberal Imperialists, led by Rosebery, Grey, Asquith and Haldane. In order to save their seats, the centre, led by Campbell–Bannerman, not only refused to denounce the Liberal Imperialists it accepted the annexation of the Boer Republic as a *fait accompli*.

Whilst he recognised that Liberal MPs might indeed lose their seats, such opportunism bode ill for the the long term viability of the party. In characteristically moralistic terms, Hobson saw moral decay and political decay going hand-in-hand. In an article significantly entitled 'The Last Chance for the Liberal Party', he argued: 'Had they [the Liberal centre in Parliament] stood firm in 1899, they would now be double strong, and the latent wisdom of the people would be rallying round them as sound men of staunch proved principle.'[32] The party, in sacrificing its principles, had lost the confidence of the electorate. In *Imperialism* he wrote: the Party's leaders in selling their party 'to a confederacy of stock gamblers and jingo sentimentalists' and in finding themselves 'impotent to defend Free Trade, Free Press, Free Schools, Free Speech, or any of the rudiments of ancient Liberalism', had 'alienated the confidence of the people'.[33]

Although at the outbreak of the war he had attributed the party's overt or tacit acquiescence in imperialism to electoral opportunism, he now put it down to its social composition. He held that its

> position as a buffer party between the propertied classes, organised as Conservatism and the unorganised pressure of a loose set of forces striving to become a socialist Labour party dictates moderation and the personnel of its leaders still drawn from the propertied classes prevents it from making any bold attempt to work Imperialism upon the basis of direct taxation upon property...[34]

Until January 1901 he still entertained the hope that the Liberal Party could be won to the progressive cause. At his prompting, a meeting was held at the South Place Ethical Society to discuss 'A Possible Programme for a Liberal Party',[35] although he saw the Party's commitment to imperialism as preventing it from taking social reform seriously.[36] By July 1901, however, he announced the 'death' of the Liberal Party, probably as a result of the divisions caused by Campbell-Bannerman's 'methods of barbarism' speech in June 1901, which brought the Liberal Imperialists to the brink of leaving. The party had a 'dead soul'; and he asked, 'How long are we going to hamper progress by dragging along with us the body of this death?'[37] He now began to make overtures to the ILP, which had stood firm against the war. Hardie, at this juncture was out to attract left-wing Liberals. The ILP, if augmented by 'semi-Socialist Radicals', could form the 'nucleus of the Party of the future'.[38] In September 1901, Hobson opined: 'if ever the time was ripe for an effective Labour Party, it is now. The old Liberal Party is rotten to its core, divided in just as many separate ways as there are separate issues.'[39] The Taff Vale judgement would push the trade unions into politics and the ILP could provide the nucleus of a new party, provided it waived 'the assertion of certain ideals, so that there could be a "Socialisme Sans Doctrines"'.[40]

Through the pages of the *Echo*[41] in an article entitled 'A New Party', he called upon the ILP, trade union leaders and Liberals to form a new party. He wanted the trade unions to enter politics not to assert their narrow interests but on a platform that dealt with measures which would generally improve working-class living conditions, that is those concerned with the 'ownership and taxation of land, old age pensions, length of the working day and graduated taxation'.[42] At the same time, Hobson noted that certain sections of the Liberal Party wanted to 'perfect the machinery of Democracy for the attainment of social progress upon lines essentially harmonious with the Labour movement, as entailed in land reform' and 'such measures of municipal or state socialism as are necessary to secure equality of opportunities in the fullest sense'.[43] The party was not only divided on these issues but its leadership connived in Britain's imperialist venture in South Africa, and imperialism was the 'deadly enemy' of social reform. He called upon the ILP to unite with disaffected Liberals, such as himself, around a minimum programme that included such questions as taxation, land reform, nationalisation of the railways and mines, the development of municipal services and the socialisation of monopolies. And if agreement could not be reached in these areas, then at least there could be a united front against imperialism and militarism.

He called for a round-table conference, consisting of a small number of working-class, middle-class, trade unionist, Radical and socialist leaders to discuss the 'greatest level of agreement for practical politics between these groups and the question of whether this common denominator was sufficient for an alliance in the country and in Parliament'.[44]

Hobson's proposals met with a mixed reaction from various MPs, trade union and socialist leaders.[45] In terms of political significance, the most important replies came from the ILP leaders. Both Hardie and MacDonald were initially favourably disposed to the idea. But they emphatically declared that they merely wanted to establish the grounds for co-operation with Liberal dissidents, rather than establish a new party.[46] MacDonald argued that if a new party was formed immediately, suspicion would arise among trade unionists that it would be captured by the Liberal Party, just at a time when they were developing their own independent political force. Although not opposed to the idea of a progressive party in principle, for the present he wanted to develop a common understanding on immediate social reforms and on electoral strategy.[47] Hardie, it seems, was more interested in electoral co-operation with disaffected Liberals than anything else.[48] On the question of wider co-operation he presented these Liberals with a choice:

> if the Anti-War Radicals are prepared for a frank, open, and above-board working agreement with the Labour forces for certain well-defined purposes, my opinion is that they can have it. If on the other hand, they are still hankering after the fleshpots of official Liberalism, then the I.L.P. is quite fit to take care of itself single-handed in the future as it has been in the past...[49]

J. Bruce Glasier, the ILP's chairman, was the most unsympathetic to the idea of a round-table conference. He distrusted the Radical Liberals, whom he saw as too closely tied to the Liberal Party. He wished to confine co-operation merely to the issue of the war.[50] MacDonald, too, began to share Glasier's doubts about whether these Liberals would break their ties with the Liberal Party, and whether they were genuinely well-disposed to the ILP.[51]

Hobson, in replying, toned down his original demand for a new party, and merely called for a 'provisional working alliance' on 'certain specific objects', e.g., temperance, housing, imperialism and militarism. He also suggested electoral co-operation between trade unionists and 'progressives'.[52] In addition, he attempted to counter the charge that dissident Liberals were fundamentally anti-collectivist and therefore unsympathetic to the claims of labour. He maintained that the old, doctrinaire individualism was yielding to the fact that free competition was being replaced by combination, and that there was no longer any fear of real revolutionary socialism. These Liberals were also beginning to recognise the beneficial effects of trade unionism among the employers and employed, as well as the need for state intervention in industrial disputes. Thus, 'socialistic' ideas, such as old age pensions and land reform, were becoming acceptable to them.

Hardie, by the end of November, had completely cooled even to the idea of electoral co-operation, although eighteen months later he went along with a secret electoral pact with the Liberals.[52] He asserted that in effect Liberals had 'nothing in common with [the ILP's] ideals', and that the 'formation and development of character is a first requirement of all reform, and character is weakened, not strengthened, by compromises and arrangements'.[53]

After the failure of Hobson's efforts, there is little direct evidence of continuing attempts to bring a new 'progressive' party into being. However, he worked under the editorship of his friend Hobhouse on the short-lived *Tribune*. Hobhouse was an 'independent' at this time. The paper was sympathetic to the ILP and trade unionists, and called for a 'New Radical Party' in the form of the 'British Democratic Association', which would act as a ginger group on the Liberal Party on issues such as the reform of land, taxation and the constitution.[54] Nevertheless, his attention may have increasingly turned back towards the Liberal Party as it became more united (and possibly more electable) as a result of its opposition to the Tariff Reform measures proposed by Joseph Chamberlain in 1903. There was at least one issue upon which the party could unite: free trade.

Working within the Liberal Party (1906–16)

After the huge Liberal election victory in 1906, Hobson sought to affect Liberal policy through working within the party. Thus, in Hardie's phrase, he seemed to have returned to the 'fleshpots of official Liberalism'. He joined staff of the *Nation* under the editorship of H. W. Massingham in March 1907, where he remained until 1920. The magazine, Hobson later claimed, was a 'real influence in the new trend of Liberalism'.[55] It was closely connected with the Lloyd George wing of the Cabinet, and it exerted its influence through its famous, weekly 'Nation' lunches, held at the National Liberal Club. No doubt Hobson also felt that he had some reforming impact, because ten out of the twenty-five Rainbow Circle members had been elected to the 1906 Parliament. Yet Hobson during this 1906-14 period of Liberal government oscillated between optimism and despair as to what the government could and would achieve.[56] Initially, in a triumphalistic vein he thought that the government would achieve much: he wrote in an unsigned editorial in the *Nation* [57] that,

> For the first time in the history of English Liberalism, leaders with a powerful support of the rank and file have committed themselves with zeal and even passionate conviction to promote a series of practical measures which, though not closely welded in their immediate purport, have the common result of increasing the powers and resources of the state for the improvement of the material and moral condition of the people.

Liberalism, he claimed, was 'now formally committed to a task which certainly involves a new conception of the state in its relation to the individual life and to private enterprise'.[58] And, somewhat counter to many of his previous criticisms of the Liberal Party, he now argued that its lack of theoretical principles, which he had formerly associated with its opportunism, was its hidden strength in comparison to Continental liberal parties. The 'logical weakness' of British liberalism 'has been a source of practical strength. It implies at any rate an adaptability, a plasticity, perhaps an instinctive virtue of adjustment that may enable British Liberalism to avoid the shipwreck which Continental Liberalism has suffered when it was driven on the submerged reefs of the economic problem of politics.' [59]

Nevertheless, his faith in the capacity of the Liberal Party to deliver social reform was not unbounded. Although he strongly supported Lloyd George's controversial Budget of 1909, with its increased taxation of the rich, he saw this as the result of political necessity, rather than choice. The Budget and welfare measures of 1909 were 'integral parts of an earnest though tardy endeavour of the Government to recover its damaged prestige and to develop that bolder and more constructive Liberalism for the lack of which almost every Liberal party in Europe has perished'.[60] He noted that the Liberal administration in its early years had 'made a tardy recognition of its obligations in the form of employment bureaux and of relief committees under the recent Unemployment Act'.[61] And he saw that measures, such as the Trade Union Act, education, licensing and land reforms, were essentially 'conservative', i.e. merely restoring 'for that people and the state, liberties or privileges, which had within recent generations been lost or encroached upon by some class, trade, or other vested interest'.[62]

Hobson saw the party's tardiness on the social front as demonstrating that it was undergoing a deep crisis. Could it put 'organic' policies into practice? In the shadow of the conflict over the Budget with the House of Lords he wrote:

> Will Liberalism, reformed and dedicated to this new, enlarged and positive task of realising liberty, carry its adherents with unbroken ranks, with persistent vigour along this march of social progress? The

real crisis of Liberalism lies here ... in the intellectual and moral ability to accept and execute a positive policy which involves a new conception of the functions of the state.[63]

Unless the 'larger body of the party' could be won over, the party was 'doomed to the same sort of impotence that has already befallen Liberalism in most Continental countries'.[64] This was 'the last chance for English Liberalism'.[65] Hobson and others such as Lloyd George, Masterman and C. P. Scott, were apprehensive about the Liberal Party being outflanked by a socialist–labour party on the question of social reform. The Liberal 'centre' was the real problem. It lacked 'passion and principle' and was 'continually disposed to ennervating compromise'.[66] Hobson employed his old 'money-bags' explanation. The weakness of the 'centre' stemmed from its social base, especially in Parliament, where it consisted of 'well-to-do people whose social policy is weakened by fears of high taxation and of encroachments upon private profitable enterprise'.[67] Liberals outside Parliament were equally unenthusiastic about social reform: 'holding as they do, a difficult and slippery footing in some business or profession, they are nervous about attacks on property, disturbances of business, bureaucracy, corruption, mob domination'.[68] As we have already seen, one of his main political tasks was to allay these fears, through fusing liberal and socialist principles. And in parliamentary terms, in order to stiffen the party's reforming resolve he, and other new Liberals, saw the Labour Party as having an important part to play as a ginger group.[69]

The need for Labour, and more generally for the working class to firm up the resolution of the Liberal Party seemed to Hobson even more urgent as a result of the Government's failure in government to crush the Curragh Mutiny in 1914 and to denounce Tory collusion in it. In his polemic *Traffic in Treason* he attributed this inability to its middle-class nature.[70] The Liberal Party would not be equal to the struggle for 'democracy' (i.e. the abolition of the House of Lords veto, and the democratisation of the army and civil service), 'unless the organised working people of this country in the Labour Party and in their trade unions can be brought to stiffen , and if necessary to direct Liberalism, there is little hope of victory'.[71] Thus, the party had to 'liberate itself from the narrowness of its outlook, the unreality of its attitude, and the timidity of its methods. It can only do this by calling in the more active assistance of those people who it has professed to "trust", but has always sought to "manage".'[72] C. P. Scott, in commenting on this tract to Hobhouse, felt that for Hobson, 'the existing Liberal Party is played out and that if it is to count for anything in the future, it must be constructed largely on a labour basis'.[73]

We should note that ,although Hobson was primarily concerned with the party's attitude to social reform in this period, he was acutely aware of the interrelationship between foreign and domestic issues, and he felt that certain aspects of its foreign policy and its attitude to militarism left much to be desired. At a protest meeting against the Anglo-Russian Entente held at the South Place Ethical Society, he objected not only to the content of the government's policy but also to the way in which it was formulated. He demanded that the government stop 'financing the butchers of Riga', and that 'English foreign policy must not continue to be the secret policy of our Foreign Office, but must be the policy of English democracy. This is a moral question that lies at the root of civilisation.'[74] Later in 1912, in a series of articles he wrote with H. N. Brailsford entitled 'The Trend of Foreign Policy', he criticised the party for its involvement in power politics, and rebuked it because it had 'utterly failed in the constructive tasks of peace; we have made an inheritance which must issue either in the slavery of conscription or the curse of war'.[75] Finally, he rejected the Liberal government's armaments policy. In reviewing the history of its recent stance on this question in 1914, he objected to Haldane's justification of the Army Estimates of 1906. 'It was not a question of meeting obligations incurred by the late Government' that explained the size of the estimates, but 'a deliberate assuming of new obligations of a similar order'.[76]

Leaving the Liberals and joining Labour (1916 and after)

If the Liberal Party's handling of the Curragh Mutiny did much to undermine his faith in the party, its policies during the First World War were ultimately decisive. The Liberal government passed the Defence of the Realm Act in September 1914, which infringed the freedoms of speech, press and assembly, and made possible arrest and imprisonment without trial. For Hobson, the British state seemed to have become as bad as the 'Prussian' state that it was fighting.[77] Naturally, he also sharply disagreed with Liberal foreign policy. He found himself in the same position as he had during the Boer War, when he was at loggerheads with 'official' Liberalism. For reasons of state it had jettisoned its fundamental principles. Again, many socialists and certain sections of the labour movement proved to be almost his only true allies. After he had failed to persuade the Liberal government to adopt a policy of neutrality at the beginning of the war, through the Neutrality Group, composed of himself, Lord Courtney, Lowes Dickenson, Graham Wallas, Gilbert Murray and Lord Bryce, he devoted his campaigning energies to the Union of Democratic Control (UDC). This body aimed to bring about a negotiated peace and to promote the democratic control of foreign policy. The last straw, as far as his commitment to the Liberal Party was concerned, came in 1916. The Coalition government formed in May 1915, headed first by Asquith and then by Lloyd George, proposed in 1916 to abandon the great historic liberal principle, free trade, in prosecution of the war. The government intended protection to last not just for the duration of the war, but after it as well. Hobson's book, entitled

The New Protectionism can be seen in a sense as a justification of his abandonment of the party.

Although he did not immediately join the Labour Party, he became firmly part of the 'Lib–Lab' milieu during the war. The UDC was composed mainly of ILPers and Liberals, and it served as a 'bridge' for many Liberals who joined either the Labour Party or the ILP.[78] And Hobson, along with H. W. Nevinson, founded the 1917 Club, which, although ostensibly established to commemorate the Russian Revolution of Febuary 1917, 'was planned to be a point of rapprochement for Liberal and Labour people who felt the same way about the war'.[79] In this period, along with other disaffected Liberals, he did not see the small and apparently doctrinaire ILP or the Labour Party as an immediately attractive proposition.[80]

In the 1918 elections, Hobson stood as an independent candidate for the Combined Universities seat. Significantly, in his manifesto he gave general support to the Labour Party. In this period, until 1924, he remained close to the Party, but did not consent to be strictly bound by it.[81] Eventually he joined the Labour Party, almost by default. The Liberal Party no longer seemed a viable proposition, either electorally or in terms of principle. He never, though, felt quite at home in the Labour Party, 'in a body governed by trade union members and their finance, and intellectually led by full-blooded socialists'.[82] Moreover, he was strongly critical of its 'opportunism'.[83] It was, indeed, only 'formally'[84] or 'nominally' socialist.[85] Nevertheless, this did not stop him trying to win the party over to his ideas. He collaborated with Brailsford, Creech Jones and E. F. Wise to produce, in 1926, *The Living Wage*, for the ILP, although he was not a member. In this document his underconsumptionist analysis strongly featured. It was debated at the Labour Party conference the following year, but was, as we have noted in Chapter one, effectively lost in committee.[86]

At the same time, consistent with his Lib–Lab strategy, he

continued to press for co-operation between the Liberal and Labour parties. In July 1924 he and C. P. Scott saw Ramsay MacDonald, now the Labour Prime Minister of a minority government, and attempted to mitigate his hostility to the Liberals in Parliament .[87] In the following year he advocated co-operation between the parties on the land question.[88] And in the subsequent year he called for a joint approach on foreign policy, minimum wages and public control of basic industries.[89] Again, in 1928, he pleaded that both parties co-operate in the elections of the following year. He argued that this was necessary because the Liberal Party's programme 'Britain's Industrial Future', which could be said 'to mark a new era of Liberalism',[90] might attract Labour voters to the Liberal Party, and thereby letting the Tories win. A year later, when it looked as though Labour would not get an absolute majority, he suggested that Labour ought to enlist Liberal support. Ignoring the grip that old-style Liberals had on the party, he opined:

> old *laissez-faire* Liberalism has virtually disappeared, and the measures of public control over capital and industry to which the Liberal Party is committed, are so essentially 'socialistic' that only personal sentiments and party prejudices bar the way to this evolution in free co-operation.[91]

Conclusion

His strategy, then, over the years was remarkably consistent. In its essentials, whether working within, or close to the Liberal or Labour parties, or outside both, it remained the same. It emerged from the crisis of 1890s Liberalism, when the Liberal Party seemed on the verge of collapse, to be superseded, at least in the long term, by some sort of socialist–labour party. The objective of his reform programme was to unite the efforts of social reformers and bring about some form of co-operation between middle-class progressives and working-class socialists and trade unionists. At the same time, he calculated that his programme was realisable only if this 'union of progressive forces' was achieved. Otherwise the forces of reaction would remain ascendant.

Such an alignment could only come about, Hobson felt, if, first, social reformers saw their particular panaceas within a broader understanding of the workings of society, and the significance of the 'unproductive' surplus; and, secondly, if both the middle and working classes, in part, transcended their sectional self-interests. He criticised the Liberal Party for its 'middle-classness', just as much as the Labour Party for its domination by trade union finances and priorities. Indeed, the unity of these progressive forces was not for Hobson purely instrumental. It stemmed from his 'organic' vision of society, in which each class and occupation should harmoniously work for the common good. His continual emphasis on the 'organic', interconnected nature of society aimed at overcoming this class particularism.

What made Hobson's notion of praxis so different from the Marxist interpretation lay precisely in this conception of society. He did not foresee workers becoming a 'universal' or 'hegemonic' class that could run society for the benefit of all as the result of a class struggle which transformed their consciousness. Rather, he analysed praxis within a communitarian framework, with all classes of society contributing their specialisms and talents to society as a whole. Thus, experts remained experts and workers remained workers. And in his scheme of things, middle-class 'experts', rather than workers were the potential 'universal' class, although he believed that individual members of the working class, as a result of educational reform, could become members of this expert class. Hobson had, what could be called a praxis without the 'dialectic'.

7 Hobson: yesterday and today

So far I have sought to demonstrate how Hobson's 'system' and strategy can be seen as a response to the crisis of late nineteenth-century British liberalism. His objective was to synthesise liberal and socialist values and explanations in order to create the theoretical foundations of a 'progressive' middle- and working-class alliance, which, he hoped, would eventually defeat the forces of reaction. There are, nevertheless, at least two questions still outstanding. How coherent was his theoretical synthesis? And what is his historical significance, in particular his relation to the liberal tradition, his intellectual influence and his contemporary relevance?

Historical significance

Hobson's historical significance can be assessed in two ways: in terms of his intellectual impact upon others; and his relationship with the liberal tradition.

Hobson and the liberal tradition

Can it be claimed that Hobson worked wholly within the liberal tradition to such an extent that in later life his 'liberalism strengthened and matured.'[1]

First, we have to avoid the danger of attempting to settle the question by definitional fiat. For example, an individual is a liberal because s/he defined themselves as such, or were described by others as such.[2] This definition poses a problem in Hobson's case, because he was quite happy to describe the policies he advocated as 'progressive socialism'[3] or 'practicable socialism'.[4] Indeed, the crucial distinction for Hobson was just as much between 'practical' and 'theoretical' socialism, as between liberalism and socialism.[5] Although his core explanations and prescriptions remained fairly constant over time, the epithet he chose to describe his policies was, in fact, remarkably inconsistent. Whether this was the product of loose thinking or the result of his aim to create a 'progressive' alliance, by telling socialists that they were really liberals , and liberals they were really socialists, we do not know. In *The Crisis of Liberalism* he could simultaneously imply that his conception of the state was 'not Socialism'[6] and that it was 'practicable Socialism'.[7] He could describe the principle of equality of opportunity as socialist,[8] or as liberal.[9] He even saw Sydney Webb's 'fourfold path' of socialism as 'constructive liberalism'.[10]

The question of Hobson's affinity with the liberal tradition is better resolved at the conceptual level. The burden of this study has been to show how Hobson sought to effect a genuine fusion of liberal and socialist principles in order to construct a middle-working-class 'progressive' alliance. This led him to depart from traditional liberal principles in a number of crucial respects, which makes it difficult to portray Hobson as consistently developing the liberal tradition from *within*. For example, his organic theory of society led him to argue that the 'rights' of 'Society' were just as important as those of the individual. Indeed, he asserted that individual rights only became intelligible and legitimate when seen in the context of a society, regarded as an 'organic', interdependent whole. Of equal significance, Hobson's organicism reversed the traditional liberal order of priority: the 'whole', i.e. society, ultimately took precedence over the 'parts', i.e. the individual. This was really the sub-text of the debate between him and Hobhouse about ontological individualism. Even when Hobson is at his most 'liberal', it is important to examine the precise terms in which he couched his argument. For example, the curtailment of individual rights during the First World War supposedly led to a '"rediscovery" of the importance of individual liberty'.[11] His argument against conscription, however, was not couched in traditional liberal, individualist language, but in terms of communal benefit: 'There is a net economy of political strength and progress in encouraging the free play of personal views and sentiments even when they impede the smooth activity of some particular State function.'[12] Indeed, Hobson never possessed the inveterate liberal 'suspicion' of the state as such. Rather, he was suspicious of particular *forms* of state in which the mass of the population could not democratically participate.[13] An undemocratic state also strengthened the forces of reaction, and therefore impeded social reform. This was one of his key arguments against the loss of individual liberty during the First World War.[14]

For Hobson, the democratisation of the state was, moreover, designed to achieve something quite illiberal: the operationalisation of a 'general will'. This was not only in order to promote a greater sense of responsible citizenship.[15] In a truly democratic state, he held that wrong-doers would have to be 'forced to be free' in the interests of the community.[16] As we have seen, he recommended compulsory arbitration in industrial disputes that badly affected the interests of the community at large.[17] And we have already noted the illiberal tendencies in his eugenic prescriptions. His advocacy of the state regulation of sexual relations is described by Freeden as an 'astonishing statement for a liberal'.[18] It is less astonishing if seen as part of Hobson's organicism that subordinated the part to the whole, which we have seen revealed in another context in his attitude towards the 'lower races'. His illiberal tendencies were not the product of intellectual inconsistency but stemmed from his general opposition to ontological individualism, in favour of a holistic perspective: 'Society' was an entity separate from the individuals who comprised it, and equally capable of 'self-realisation'. For this reason, he saw communal welfare as possessing a value independent of its members. So he viewed the family, for instance, as the community 'writ small', as having a value *per se* as a sound well-living prosperous, serviceable stock. I cling to this ... value and will not have it dissipated into the several personal values of the particular members of this family, past, present and to come.'[19] Even liberals who were personally and politically close to Hobson, such as Hobhouse, would not follow him down this ontological road.

All this is not to suggest that there were not crucial liberal elements in Hobson's thought, such as his advocacy of competition (although he was ambivalent on this), incentives, and the need to draw clear boundaries between the state and 'civil' society. Rather, the argument is that his thought is not reducible to a liberal 'essence'. His life's intellectual project was genuinely a syncretic one: he sincerely strove to synthesise liberal and socialist values through his organic perspective. His impact on the younger generation of socialist intellectuals - Brailsford, Cole, Tawney and Laski – can be better understood by recognising just how genuine was this attempt at synthesis. They saw their socialism as the heir of liberalism, and yet qualitatively different from it. Therefore, it is more accurate to see Hobson not as a good example of the self-transformative capacities of liberalism but, instead, as an important figure in the evolution of the British social democratic tradition, which can be characterised by its compounding of socialist and liberal concepts, values and ideals.

Hobson's intellectual influence

Making any historical assessment in terms of a thinker's influence is fraught with difficulty. There is the danger of inflating the reputation of the 'subject' – the occupational disease of the intellectual biographer. And the very notion of 'influence' is tricky, if only because of the problem in estimating with any precision the degree of impact of one thinker upon another. There is the 'great man' approach followed by T. W. Hutchinson, who states that the 1945 Labour government's policies of full employment and nationalisation 'followed Hobson's ideas very closely, and these ideas may well go down as the most important single intellectual inspiration of the particular phase of British economic history and policy'.[20] Yet such a perspective underplays the extent to which knowledge is invariably a collective product. Not only do existing generations rest on the 'intellectual' shoulders of past generations, people learn from each other through discussion and debate. Thus, before the First World War, Hobson's thought and its effect is better understood if it is viewed as part of a 'progressive' intellectual and political current. It embraced in the 1890s the left wing of the Liberal Party and the ILP, the Rainbow Circle, the Fabian Society and the South Place Ethical Society, and in terms of propaganda, the *Manchester Guardian*, the *Daily Chronicle* and the *Speaker*. The dominant impulse behind this movement was the desire for social reform through an extension of the boundaries of the state into the economic realm. By and large, members of this movement had a number of important ideas in common, such as organicism, evolution, the 'surplus', 'efficiency' and the need to be 'practical'. Hence, in terms of political impact, it is difficult to claim that Hobson, along with Hobhouse, was the key intellectual inspiration of the 1906–14 reforms, because these reforms were very much the product of a whole current of opinion.

Moreover, as far as direct intellectual influence is concerned, it would appear that the *Nation*, on which Hobson worked, had a collective impact, rather than its journalists having a separate individual influence. And other forces, such as electoral considerations, also merit consideration. Finally, it is difficult to identify Hobson as the inspiration of any particular measure in this period. Indeed, for the most part, he was sceptical about the achievements of a government that he regarded as rather timid. He wanted far more fundamental social reforms. Nevertheless, Hobson did have a distinguishable role within the 'progressive' movement. He, along with Hobhouse and the Fabians, probably articulated most clearly the intellectual rationale for the 1906–14 reforms. Hobson, it would seem, must have played a significant part in the 1890s and early 1900s in overcoming the traditional liberal phobia of an enlarged state. For example, his *Problems of Poverty* (1891) had gone into eight editions by 1913, T*he Problem of Unemployment* (1896) three editions by 1906. The *Evolution of Modern Capitalism* (1894) was widely read, and went into a second edition in 1906. And this is to ignore the other substantial works he produced in this period, such as *John Ruskin, Social Reformer* and *The Social Problem and Imperialism* along with countless newspaper and magazine articles.

In considering Hobson's historical impact in the inter-war period, after the collapse of the Liberal Party and the rise of the Labour Party, again it would be questionable to assert, for example, that he was primarily responsible for giving British socialism a 'liberal face', as the *Manchester Guardian* obituary implied.[21] First, other liberal intellectuals either joined, or supported the Labour Party in the 1920s, such as R. B. Haldane, E. D. Morel, A. Ponsonby, C. P. Trevelyan and C. R. Buxton. Secondly, although the early leaders of the Labour Party saw themselves as socialists, their real differences with the Liberal Party had less to do with its ideology and more to do with seeing it as an employers' party.[22] They were anti-Liberal, rather than anti-liberal, especially in the case of MacDonald, and generally they saw their socialism as the heir of liberalism, rather than as sharply antithetical to it. Finally, although in this period the key Labour intellectuals, such as Laski, Cole, Tawney and Brailsford, had a 'liberal face', it would be hard to argue that they were Hobson 'clones', despite the fact that they held him in high regard,[23] Indeed, Hobson was never in any period of his life what Marx had been to many of his followers: no one swallowed his ideas whole. Perhaps the individual who came closest to doing so was MacDonald, whose beliefs – ethicism, organicism, notion of community, underconsumptionism and stress on role of experts in the social reform process – all tended to bear the Hobson stamp.[24] Nevertheless, whilst there were few 'Hobsonites', two aspects of his 'system' did undoubtedly have an impact: his underconsumptionism and his theory of imperialism.

Underconsumptionism

This 'heresy', although never taken seriously by orthodox economists in Britain, except belatedly by Keynes in his *General Theory*[25] was fully embraced by the Independent Labour Party in the 1920s, and became something of an orthodoxy amongst the Labour left in the inter-war years. As noted in the previous chapter, it provided the theoretical linchpin of the ILP's 'Living Wage' proposals, published in September, 1926. The Labour leadership attacked it not because of its underconsumptionist philosophy, but because it feared that the ILP wanted to implement its proposals in a style which could be seen as akin to Marxist 'transitional' demands. Indeed, MacDonald and Snowden were theoretically underconsumptionist, although not practically so.[26]

Whilst the Labour left in the 1930s, especially the ILP, espoused Hobson's underconsumptionism, the Labour right, led by Evan Durbin, Hugh Dalton and Hugh Gaitskell, came increasingly under the influence of Keynes.[27] As a means to solve the unemployment problem, he emphasised the control of credit and the increase in investment, rather than income redistribution and the socialisation of industry. Although in historical terms the Keynesians could be said to have won the debate, arguably it was Hobson who paved the way for the 'Keynesian revolution', as both thinkers saw the cause of unemployment in the lack of effective demand. For G. D. H. Cole, one of Labour's leading theoreticians in the 1930s and 1940s, the Keynesian revolution was really a Hobsonian one.[28] Indeed, Cole himself did much to synthesise the ideas of both. He sought to incorporate Keynes's technical understanding of the workings of capitalism within Hobson's moral and prescriptive vision.[29]

In the United States Hobson's underconsumptionism found greater resonance even in academic circles, which, in terms of economic theory, had a far more heterogeneous tradition than the British.[30] His theory was seriously discussed by American economists as early as 1895.[31] He was perhaps at his most influential in the late 1920s–early 1930s. At least one member – R. G. Tugwell – of Roosevelt's 'Brain's Trust', which inspired the New Deal in the 1930s was strongly influenced by Hobson.[32] His works were widely reviewed in American economics journals. In the 1920s he gave lectures at such prestigious academic venues as the Brookings Institute. Some idea of Hobson's importance in this period can be gleaned from the fact that an American commentary of contemporary economic thought gave as much space to Hobson as to Marshall, Veblen, J. B. Clark and W. C. Mitchell.[33] That Hobson was taken far more seriously in American academic circles is underscored by his offer of a university post. He was never offered one in Britain. Since the Second World War quite a number of Hobson's economic works have been reprinted in the United States, such as *The Physiology of Industry, Problems of Poverty, The Economics of Distribution, International Trade, The Industrial System, , The Economics of Unemployment* and *Work and Wealth* , whereas in Britain only his autobiography, *Confessions of an Economic Heretic* (1976) and two political works have been reprinted, *The Crisis of Liberalism* (1974) and *Imperialism* (1948,1954, 1961, 1968, 1988).

Imperialism

Similarly, Hobson's theory of imperialism achieved far greater acclaim abroad than at home. Hobson has been held with some esteem in Marxist circles ever since Lenin handsomely acknowledged his debt to him in his preface to *Imperialism, the Highest Stage of Capitalism*. Estimates of Hobson's impact on Lenin vary wildly.[34] In my view Lenin used Hobson's writings to embellish a theoretical framework attributable to Hilferding and Bukharin (whom Lenin puzzlingly omits to mention in his preface). He supplied Lenin with data, not concepts. Lenin's theory underlined the irreconcilable contradictions of capitalism as a system, rather than the nefarious activities of capitalists urgent to offload the 'unproductive' surplus, which according to the Hobsonian thesis, created the necessary but not sufficient conditions for imperialism. Hobson provided Lenin with evidence to demonstrate the way in which Britain, because it was becoming a rentier state, was ceasing to be a 'progressive' capitalist economy. In addition, Lenin derived from Hobson confirmation of the existence of a labour aristocracy in Britain, as well as statistics on British trade, investment and imperial expansion.

In the United States Hobson's reputation among academic historians was established in the 1920s, when Parker Moon's influential study of the origins of the First World War, *Imperialism and World Politics* (1926) was published. Moon closely followed Hobson's conceptual framework, and even used some of Hobson's phrases.[35] Yet, although Hobson's influence on American writers on imperialism in the earlier part of the twentieth century appears to have been strong,[36] a danger exists in attributing too much to Hobson. An indigenous American, liberal, anti-monopoly tradition predates Hobson. Indeed, one of the significant figures in this tradition, H. D. Lloyd, author of *Wealth against Commonwealth* (1894), quite possibly contributed, indirectly, to Hobson's own anti-monopoly stance. William Clarke, one of the Fabian essayists who made a strong impression on Hobson in his politically and intellectually formative period in the early 1890s, was deeply influenced by Lloyd's writings on American trusts from the mid-1880s.[37] Hobson became a friend of Lloyd's, and other aspects of Hobson's writings bore the mark of Lloyd (e.g. the compromise between private and public ownership.[38] Moreover, other Americans such as Gaylord Wilshire linked the trust phenomenon with imperialism, independently of Hobson.[39] Nevertheless, Hobson could be said to have greatly contributed to this American anti-monopoly, anti-imperialist tradition, in the sense of reinforcing it. This tradition continues up to the present, if in a more Marxist idiom, in the works, for example, of Baran and Sweezy.[40]

In Britain Hobson's theory of imperialism had its followers. H. N. Brailsford, with whom Hobson closely associated on the Nation and who later became editor of the ILP's *New Leader* in the 1920s, wrote a widely influential account of the origins of the First World War, *War of Steel and Gold* (1914). He employed Hobson's analytical and prescriptive model.[41] Brailsford's work made a profound impression on MacDonald, Philip Snowden and even President Wilson in their attempts to formulate an anti-imperialist, but not an anti-capitalist foreign policy during the War.[42] Hobson's theory of imperialism, whether or not mediated through Brailsford, continued to influence Labour thinking on foreign policy in the inter-war years.[43] Even after the Second World War his ideas surfaced in works such as John Strachey's *End Of Empire* (1959). He argued, effectively within Hobson's underconsumptionist paradigm, that imperialism had been eclipsed, because the investible surplus, which had formerly sought foreign outlets, was now absorbed domestically, through income redistribution, as a result of the growth of 'democracy'.[44] Today his theory continues to excite interest and debate in academic circles, which is not surprising. After all, he, along with Lenin, was responsible for creating a new genre of historic enquiry, 'economic imperialism'.[45]

Hobson's system assessed

Michael Freeden has strongly emphasised the new liberalism's adaptability, its capacity to shake off the theoretical and political shibboleths of the old liberalism. He states: 'The new liberals constructed a powerful and coherent and relevant edifice without compromising on what was inherently liberal in their outlook'.[46] He gives Hobson a star role in this process of intellectual trans- formation. Hobson was 'by far the most original and penetrating of the new liberal theorists at the turn of the century...'[47] His perspective 'came close to consituting a coherent system, despite a number of inconsistencies'.[48] And Hobson was among a number of new liberals who 'by remaining at the same time steadfast liberals ... proved in practice the logical compatibility of liberalism and socialism.'[49] Two questions are raised here: did Hobson manage to transform liberalism, whilst remaining at the same time a 'steadfast liberal'? This question has already been considered earlier in the chapter, where we showed how Hobson in a number of crucial respects went beyond the liberal tradition, in order to bring about a fusion of liberalism and socialism. And, secondly, to what extent was Hobson's system 'coherent'? That is, how successful was Hobson in his attempts, first, to put his moral theory either on a naturalistic or an empirical footing, i.e. combining facts and values; and, secondly, to 'humanise' economic thought, which he regarded as his primary intellectual task.

His 'naturalised' ethics appeared in a number of forms. He argued that all types of parasitism would receive their natural and just retribution. Thus, in its imperialist manifestation: 'Nature is not mocked: the laws which, operative throughout nature, doom the parasite to atrophy, decay, and final extinction, are not evaded by nations any more than by individual organisms.'[50] Apart from being questionable in biological terms – that parasites necessarily decay any more rapidly than any other organisms – such a statement evades the need for historical analysis into precisely why empires decline, or, indeed, why certain empires have experienced longevity. As for social parasitism, he often employed his own rendition of Ruskin's commandment borrowed from St Paul: "Whosoever will not work, neither can he eat" is the physical rendering of the moral law. For physical diseases bred of stolen luxuries, those which spring from chronic starvation are literal counterparts.'[51] In support of this position, he quoted statistics demonstrating that 'the death rate for the "unoccupied" classes after the age of sixty is actually higher than it is for the overworked, ill-fed, worse-housed agricultural labourers.'[51] Here, Hobson failed to transcend the tendentious: even if true, this avoided making comparisons with the industrial proletariat, or considering the question of life expectancy between the 'unoccupied' and agricultural classes.

Hobson, in his discussion of parasitism also combined factual and value statements in another way. He used the terms 'unproductive' and 'unearned' surplus interchangeably.[53] His economic theory assumed that the 'unearned' surplus was necessarily 'unproductive' because it was automatically invested in capital that produced goods that could find no consumers. In other words, the hypothetically correct ratio between saving and consumption was upset. This attempted fusion of facts and values looks, however, less persuasive when considered in the light of what most economists have regarded as crucial aspects of economic life and behaviour, namely that investment does not only create demand for producer goods but also for consumer goods. Workers in industries where this extra investment has occurred will increase their consumption, either because more of them will be employed in it or because they will be getting higher wages.[54] Further, Hobson did not fully consider the role of interest rates in mediating between saving and investment. Whatever the merits or demerits of Hobson's position, to admit that unearned income was not necessarily unproductive would have considerably weakened his technical, in contrast to his moral, case for its taxation, and thereby his attempt to unite facts and values.

Finally, in urging that there existed 'natural' barriers to consumption by the rich (and that is why they invested), he undermined his own position by employing Veblen's critique of the 'conspicuous consumption' of the parasitic classes. This form of consumption could regarded in an intuitive sense as limitless.[55]

The second major consideration in analysing Hobson's 'system' is whether he managed rigorously to 'humanise' economic thought. He openly admitted that he had difficulties in realising this undertaking: first, in demarcating between economic and non-economic forms of utility; secondly in choosing between the current or an ideal criterion for measuring human value;[56] and thirdly, in comparing the pleasures and pains of one individual with another.[57] Many commentators in criticising Hobson have identified certain technical weaknesses, some of which stem from these self-confessed problems. Thus, although he expressed himself in the language of utilitarianism and tried to develop a humanistic felicific calculus, he had set himself an impossible task. In moving away from an objective, monetary and quantitative calculus towards a subjective, qualitative, one, he failed to appreciate that qualitative differences are not commensurable.[58] Differences in subjective evaluations also made the operationalisation of his principles of taxation, based on the distinction between 'costs' and 'surplus', problematic. Each individual has his or her own estimate of the utilities and disutilities of work and reward that is unlikely to accord with another's evaluation.[59] Indeed, the problem of distinguishing between costs and surpluses was compounded, because Hobson had argued, in opposition to the marginalists that, even the most marginal units accrued some form of rent.[60]

Hobson's difficulties in bringing this project to fruition, however, may be explored from another angle. They can be viewed as deriving from his general theoretical strategy of synthesising the aesthetic, humanistic values of Ruskin, with a liberal political economy, premissed upon the Benthamite hedonistic calculus.[61] He implicitly sought to integrate two conceptions of human nature: one which put the development of human aesthetic, moral and intellectual potentials at a premium; the other which saw human beings as 'infinite' consumers and appropriators.[62] Hobson was not able to transcend this difficulty, one which has dogged the liberal tradition since Mill and Green. Both philosophers had a developmental model of human nature, while simultaneously holding to the prevailing utilitarian canons of liberal political economy, with its stress on the justice and efficiency of the market.[63]

Hobson's difficulties can be highlighted by considering the means by which he proposed to realise his social ideals. These were, first, the developmental ideal, inspired principally by Ruskin, who claimed that there was as much satisfaction to be gained from producing as consuming. Progress consisted of the qualitative and quantitative reduction of individual disutilities, and the maximising of utilities, in the realms of production and consumption. Secondly, Hobson espoused an ideal of social justice. This consisted of equality of opportunity, which, as we have already noted, contained a central ambiguity. It either meant equality in competing for scarce resources or it meant equal entitlement to self-development. Social justice, for Hobson, had another distributive dimension: work and reward should be consistent with the socialist maxim 'From each according to his (or her) ability, to each according to their needs', with the latter normally defined in terms of 'social utility', i.e. an individual's capacity to contribute to the 'common good'. He believed that if the principles of social justice prevailed, then a third ideal would be achieved – social harmony. Although he held that education and opportunity to participate in civic life were important in fostering this harmony, a material basis was also vital. This required the eradication of 'improperty', the unearned surplus, through taxation and equality of opportunity. Indeed, all Hobson's social goals could be achieved only if the market economy was sufficiently reformed to eliminate as far as possible all 'unproductive' or 'unearned' surpluses.

Achieving self-development

His aim, in contrast to 'theoretical' socialists was 'not to abolish the competitive system, … but rather to supply all workers at cost price with all the economic conditions requisite to the education and employment of their personal powers for their own personal advantage and enjoyment'.[64] He wanted, therefore, to retain the market system, which would supply workers at 'cost price', while simultaneously realising human potentials. That these two goals are not necessarily compatible is underlined by Hobson's own meanings which he attached to the notion of 'cost'. One he identified with incentives, i.e. 'that part of the product, or its equivalent in other goods, necessary as payments to maintain the current output of productive energy as a factor of production'.[65] Cost here was the price of productivity. The other cost was Ruskin-inspired. For example, when noting the harmful effects of the division of labour and machinery, he observed that the 'economic "cost of production" of commodities is reduced to a minimum,' whilst the 'real human cost is continually enhanced'.[66] Thus, a tension arose between cost defined as the quantitative goal of productivity for 'social utility', and cost viewed in a qualitative, humanistic light, directly related to the effects of production (and consumption) upon a worker's existence.

Hobson assumed that a reformed market, through the regulation of working conditions, and, in the long term, the increased use of machinery, would reduce human costs. But the problem remains: given his attachment to productivity and incentives, there could be no guarantee that human costs would be minimised in general. Individuals might undertake certain jobs because of the pecuniary incentive to do so, despite the subjective costs, for instance either to health or self-realisation. Although Hobson clearly advocated some regulation of subjective costs, the loss of self-realisation was not among them, at least in the short term. Indeed, in considering the relationship between rewards and incentives, on the one hand, and human costs, on the other, it is quite conceivable that a high wage could induce individuals to do less work owing to the high subjective costs. Or a reduced wage could stimulate greater productivity, and greater human cost, because individuals may have to work harder to achieve the same earnings. Thus, his general assumption that greater rewards would lead to greater individual productivity was gratuitous.[67] Further, because Hobson normally identified 'social utility' with productivity, he paid little attention to the possibility that, in aggregate terms, lower productivity could be associated with greater subjective satisfaction. Neither did he grapple in the short term with the question of boring jobs, although in the long term he believed that their impact could be attenuated through the use of machinery that would reduce the length of the working day. In the meantime he merely accepted the need to pay a sufficient amount to workers to induce them to perform these tasks.[68] As to whether workers undertaking these tasks should be compensated by increased leisure, which he regarded as the 'opportunity of opportunities',[69] Hobson was decidedly ambiguous. On the one hand, he could approve of this, to offset the 'human' costs of the division of labour.[70] Yet, on the other hand, he saw that this would 'signify great waste of communal opportunities. For there is no natural adjustment between the longer leisure for scavengers or coalminers and the shorter leisure for gardners and teachers with regard to their respective capacity to use their leisure.'[71] Even if we accept Hobson's estimate of the different capacities of these groups to use their leisure fruitfully, he clearly ignores the possibility that coalminers and scavengers, if given sufficient resources in terms of income and education, would be able to use their leisure for self-developmental purposes in a way not directly related to their jobs. Indeed, in this argument, he does not consider their right to be able to do so.

In *Work and Wealth* he proposed a further solution to the problem of unpleasant jobs. He adopted what could be termed the 'Hegelian' strategy of making the 'real' appear 'rational'. He wanted to change the consciousness of workers in the socialised 'routine' industries. Although their jobs were intrinsically boring, they would no longer resent this fact, once they recognised that they were part of a grand collective project, in which 'Society' would realise itself.[72]

Thus, although in the long term Hobson hoped to solve the problem of the lack of self-realisation for the mass of the population through the increased use of machinery that would increase leisure time, in the short term, whilst he accepted the need to establish a 'living wage' and maximum working hours, the market would largely determine the distribution of work and reward, and therefore the possibilities for self-realisation. He therefore failed to transcend the dualistic account of human nature, bequeathed by Mill and Green, as self-developer, or as infinite consumer or appropriator. The market remained essential for 'efficiency' or 'social utility'.

Achieving social justice

Hobson also held that the reform of the market would promote social justice. The opening up of the educational system and the socialisation of the monopolies would help create equality of economic opportunity. With the market reformed, the unproductive surpluses would be eliminated, and his 'needs' formula would come into operation. We have already noted that his dual commitment to liberal political economy and the Ruskinian self-developmental vision led him to use the term equality of opportunity in a double sense, i.e. as equality to compete (procedural) and equality to self-realise (substantive). Clearly, there is no necessary congruity between these two meanings. For example, a loser in a competition for a job that offered possibilities for self-realisation could be said to have been dealt with fairly on procedural grounds, if the the competition was fair, but not on substantive grounds, assuming that the job could have greatly contributed to the loser's self-realisation.

His attempt to marry liberal and Ruskinian political economy created further problems in equitably allocating work and rewards. As we have seen, his 'needs' formula was in essence a productivity formula. 'Social utility' required that individuals were paid according to their powers, i.e. the amount and type of power expended.[73] In effect, this meant that the middle-class professions would get more than the working classes because the jobs they performed required that they be given 'provision for the continuous stimulation and satisfaction of new powers and interests'.[74] Hence, 'a higher-grade worker should have a higher rate of pay than a low-grade worker, because his "needs" are greater, and since these needs can only be properly supplied by private expenditure, he ought to have a larger property'.[75] Professional people would, therefore, not only receive greater rewards than manual workers they would also have more interesting jobs. However, he argued that this inequity could be mitigated by widening educational provision so that there would be more competition for the interesting jobs, causing wages to fall in this sector, and less willingness to perform arduous and/ or boring jobs, causing wages to rise in this sector.[76] But this solution is problematic in a number of ways. There will still be winners and losers, which is inherent in the nature of competition, as there is no guaranteed 'fit' between the number of interesting jobs and the number willing and able to do them. And, furthermore, if interesting jobs were in short supply, all that would happen, if there were a more educated workforce, would be that the wages attached to interesting jobs would fall, and the losers would have to do the boring jobs, which therefore would prevent wages from rising in this sector, and probably increase the dissatisfaction of educated people having to do this type of work.

In addition, it could be argued that it is precisely because workers in 'routine' industries get little chance of self-realisation through their jobs that they need greater wealth and leisure to realise themselves outside their jobs. Finally, Hobson's market solution to the problems of social justice was effectively ruled out by himself, since he argued that 'markets are instrinsically unfair modes of distribution',[77] because 'nowhere are the bargaining powers of supply and demand on an equal footing, and everywhere individual buyers and sellers, whether of goods and services, are so unequal in their 'need' to sell and buy that the advantage accruing from sales at any given price give widely different advantages to those who participate'.[78] This critique of the market he regarded as his most 'destructive heresy'.[79]

Achieving social harmony

Hobson aimed to promote social harmony at the ideological and political level through an appropriately humanistic education, as well as through the democratisation of the political process. At the material level, he recognised that this entailed an equitable distribution of the surplus. For the root cause of industrial conflict lay in the existence of this surplus:

> Consciously, or unconsciously, every form of industrial conflict, between capital and labour in a particular industry or business, between sheltered and unsheltered, combined and competitive trades, between skilled and unskilled, organised or unorganised labour, turns eventually upon claims upon the surplus wealth which modern methods of production turn out in excess of what is economically employed in production.[80]

Where there was no surplus there was no conflict: 'So far as subsistence wages and minimum payments for capital and ability are concerned, industrial harmony exists.'[81] This was because, 'There is ... no true discepancy of interests in regard to the portion of those proceeds of a business which are entitled to rank as costs of labour, capital or ability.'[82]

He seemed unafraid of where his logic took him. Flying in the face of historical fact he stated that industrial harmony existed in the period of *laissez-faire* capitalism, and was shattered by the arrival of combination.

> Enough has been said to indicate the nature of the structural changes in modern industry and their psychological reactions which have brought about a collapse of the unseen, unconscious harmony of selfish interests that sustained the industrial system and provided a fairly effective government during the nineteenth century.[83]

The growth of combinations, 'based as they are on considerations of narrow group interest', meant that there was 'no security of peace or prosperity to the community at large'.[84] This belief in the immanent harmony of interests during the period of *laissez-faire* capitalism raises all sorts of problems for his attempted 'humanisation' of political economy, quite apart from his bizarre display of historical amnesia.

First, his notion of interests is rather limited. He assumes that the 'real' interests of workers and capitalists were in harmony with each other during the *laissez-faire* phase of capitalism. Yet this is to ignore the compulsively competitive nature of capitalism, which continually forces capitalists to drive down their costs *vis-à-vis* other capitalists, quite often to the detriment of workers as workers, however much they might benefit as consumers. Indeed, we have already noted his critique of the intrinsic inequities of the market, of the morally corrosive nature of competion: 'Selfishness is inherent in competition; force is inherent in bargaining.'[85] Secondly, his notion of 'interest' here totally ignores what he has to say elsewhere about the subjective side of the labour process, and the need to see work as a means to self-realisation, and not merely as a means to consumption as traditional liberal political economy assumes. Occasionally, he acknowledged that the lack of self-realisation could lead to industrial conflict:

> Long hours, minute subdivision of labour, mechanical routines are ... 'inhuman' [i.e. humans were not biologically intended for such work].

So far as they are required to enter into the activity of workers, problems of discipline continue to press. 'Spirited workers' will no longer 'put up with' the encroachments upon their humanity which habit and economic necessity formerly induced them to accept.[86]

To have extended this analysis, however, would have upset his causal system, with the unproductive surplus at its centre, for a conflict of 'needs' could arise, between the worker as 'self-developer', and worker as consumer, or between workers as 'self-developers' and the interests of capitalists in profit-making.

True, Hobson believed that in the long run modern technology would reduce the hard drudgery of certain forms of work and create more leisure time,[87] thereby minimising human costs. Yet this did little to solve within his own framework the problem of industrial conflict in the sense that there would still exist, according to Hobson's distributive criteria, the potential for conflict between the workers by 'hand' and 'brain'. The former would be performing creatively unrewarding tasks for lower pecuniary rewards than the latter whose 'needs' as producers were greater, and who could also be rewarded by 'prize money'. Secondly, the market, with all its conflict-inducing qualities, would continue to exist. There was still plenty of scope for the invisible hand to become a palpable fist, even if state regulation had removed the knuckle-dusters.

Hobson today

Despite these theoretical difficulties, Hobson's overall perspective has retained a relevance, often missing from his 'progressive' contemporaries. Ironically, whilst the scope, tenor and trajectory of his thought, with its sinuous and sustained critique of *laissez-faire* in all its manifestations (despite his illusions about a 'golden age' of *laissez-faire*), were shaped by the political and intellectual crisis of late nineteenth-century liberalism, his works can be of some use in the reworking of late twentieth-century socialism, which has been undergoing a similar 'crisis', both East and West. This 'crisis' is manifested in socialism's seeming lack of coherence, identity, direction and political support. Moreover, the minimal statism of the neo-liberal right seems to have assumed the moral high-ground of freedom, and socialism appears as an imperfect second best, calling for the restriction of individual liberty in the name of equality. The result has been that many socialists have come to accept the terms, if not the conclusions, of the minimalist argument.

Admittedly, Hobson's 'system' falls far short of supplying socialists with ready-made panaceas. Yet his arguments against minimal statism and for an enlarged (and reformed) state, his attempts to combine liberal and socialist principles, and, indeed, the way in which he *thought* about societal problems are all highly pertinent. His work suggests areas where socialists might look in order to defend, and persuade others of, their principles and prescriptions. To appreciate fully Hobson's contemporary resonance, we should bear in mind that he devoted a good deal of his life to addressing an essential and perplexing question: whither modern industrialism? In a sense, Hobson's work is a reminder of how little fundamental social, economic and political relations, and, indeed, arguments, have progressed in the past century, despite the breath-taking march of the machine. At bottom, his objective, as was Marx's, was to transform the machine from oppressor into an agent of human liberation. For Hobson, this necessitated a fundamental change of the economic and political relations in which the machine operated. In his solution, the enlargement of the productive and distributive activities of the state was central.

His arguments in support of this remedy merit serious consideration, especially in the light of the minimal statist case, resurrected in the writings of neo-liberal Americans, such as

Murray and Meade.[88] They argue that an 'undeserving poor' exists. Echoing the old COS perspective, they maintain that poverty is the result of 'character', of individual motives and dispositions. Thus, the state cannot be responsible in resource terms for alleviating this form of poverty. Hobson mounted a powerful assault on the highly individualistic assumptions upon which this position stands. The right to private property, and especially the machine-generated surplus element within it, could not be an absolute right, because wealth was the product of social, or 'organic', co-operation. Poverty was not the result of the moral failings of the individual. Rather, it stemmed from the economic structure. And the minimalist justification of state expenditure on the basis of advancing and protecting individual interests, which rested on the ontological individualist presupposition that society consisted merely of individuals, overlooked the fact that society was more than the sum total of its citizens and had 'its' own needs.

Hobson also propounded relevant arguments against the minimalist rejection of the socialisation of industry – what we could term the 'socialisation question'. His discussion of the socialisation of the machine hinged primarily on his distinction between quantitative and qualitative human needs. This distinction enabled him to justify socialisation on grounds that closely resembled Marx's discussion of communism in the *Grundrisse*. It provided the necessary basis for the satisfaction of qualitative needs. State ownership of the machine would facilitate the efficient satisfaction of quantitative needs, thereby increasing the leisure time – the 'opportunity of opportunities'. Thus, the working population would be able to individuate more readily, i.e. satisfy its qualitative productive and consumptive needs. Hobson was, in effect, calling for the abridging of the 'procedural' freedom of private ownership (for the few) in order to increase the substantive freedoms of the many. Put another way: he could be interpreted as challenging neo-liberal individualism by invoking the principle of individuality. The regulation and control of industry had, therefore, a powerful emancipatory potential.

His argument concerning the need to regulate machine production is relevant for another reason. For him, it was essential in order to provide the material basis for citizenship. Without increased leisure time political participation would be impeded. This would seem to be germane to recent discussions on the question of citizenship taking place inside and outside the Labour Party, which have been a response to the process of class dealignment. Appeals to class interest are seen as ineffectual. Instead there has to be an invocation of some morally based notion of the common good.[89]

Equally, his differentiation between quantitative and qualitative needs, enabling him to set clear boundaries for state encroachments into economic life, has contemporary resonance. He urged that the state should only concern itself with the socialisation of monopolistic machine industries catering for 'routine' quantitative needs (as well as with natural monopolies). It had no business interfering in productive activities designed to meet qualitative needs. What Hobson has to say on this matter is worthy of serious consideration in the light of discussions on the relation between 'plan' and 'market' taking place in the East and West. This issue all too easily can become too narrowly focused upon questions of productive efficiency. Indeed, Perry Anderson has been prompted to comment that 'Hobson's discussion both of the reasons for, and the limits to, socialisation of the means of production, has a strikingly modern ring.'[90] In fact, there are surprising parallels between Hobson's conception of a dual economy and Andre Gorz's post-industrial utopia, which rests upon a distinction between 'autonomous' and 'heteronomous' forms of productive activity.[91]

Hobson's approach to the question of socialisation is important for another reason. His liberal distrust of bureaucracy meant that, while he appreciated both its necessity and desirability, he wanted to ensure that an enlarged state was still responsive to the wishes of citizens and workers within state-owned industries. Consequently, he saw the need to bring the state and society closer together through the development of different forms of participative machinery. Whatever the merits of his particular proposals, some sort of broad-based industrial democracy in this sphere would enable socialist proposals for the socialisation of industry to command greater popular support.

Finally, some of Hobson's intellectual coinage ought to be put back into circulation, because of the *way* in which he thought about society and its problems. Although parts of his organicist position appear dated, his holistic perspective is a useful reminder to socialists and social reformers in seeing the interconnection of social problems. His totalising viewpoint meant, for example, that poverty and unemployment could not be fully understood without appreciating the pattern of income distribution and the ownership of wealth and how this affected economic fluctuations. And the question of wealth and income distribution, in Hobson's eyes, could not be separated from the need to bring about greater democracy; otherwise the wealthy would be able to employ undemocratic measures to defend their privileges. Yet democratic reform was insufficient without an improvement in civic awareness and responsibility. Moreover, questions of domestic policy could not be separated from those of foreign policy. Indeed, his holism led him to stress the interdependence of nations, and to call for a world state with executive powers.

This recognition of the interconnection of social, economic and political issues lay behind his attack on the notion that disciplines within the social sciences could be completely autonomous. His holism also came into play when criticising the certain analytic propensities of social scientists. He rejected the 'either/or' approach. His quasi-Hegelian position on methodological issues induced him to accept the irreducibility of theoretical categories, but not their irreconcilability. Thus, he could not accept a fundamental separation between facts and values within the social sciences. Facts had a moral significance. He could not stomach the pretensions of those who hid their ideologies and interests behind a façade of scientific impartiality. Just as crucially, facts not only had a moral import. They contained a practical imperative. Hobson, through his writings and by his political engagement, points the guilty finger at all those who seek to live comfortably within the moral vacuum of an academic discipline, surrounded by a hermetically sealed universe of theory.

Notes

Chapter 1

1 'J. A. Hobson', *New Statesman*, 56, 5 July 1958, p. 12.

2 *The Social Problem*, London, Nisbet, 1901, p. 4.

3 Cf. John Gray, 'The Relevance of Consent', *Times Higher Educational Supplement*, 10 November 1989, p. 18.

4 J. A. Hobson, *Confessions of an Economic Heretic*, London, Allen and Unwin, 1938, p. 15 (*CEH* hereafter).

5 Cf. *CEH*, p. 26.

6 J. M. Keynes, *The General Theory of Employment, Interest and Money*, London, Macmillan, 1936, p. 365.

7 Whether this desire for such recognition was stimulated by his elder brother's obvious academic success at Cambridge, we do not know.

8 The historical significance of this Circle should become readily apparent when we note the future careers of many of its members. Ramsay MacDonald became leader of the Labour Party and Prime Minister in the Labour governments of 1924, and 1929, as well as the Coalition government of 1931; Samuel became leader of the Liberal Party in the early 1930s; Trevelyan became a Minister in the Liberal governments of 1906-14, and then in the Labour governments of 1924 and 1929; Olivier, Governor of Jamaica in 1907, and Secretary of State for India in 1924; Reeves the High Commissioner for New Zealand in 1905, and Director of the London School of Econics in 1908; Gooch became a leading historian and Hirst a well-known Liberal journalist on economic affairs; Alden a Liberal MP in 1906; and Hammond an eminent journalist and renowned for his writings on social and economic conditions in eighteenth- and nineteenth-century Britain. Pease, along with Clarke, Olivier and Reeves, were prominent Fabians.

9 *Manchester Guardian*, 2 April 1940.

10 H. W. Nevinson, *More Changes, More Chances*, London, Nisbet, 1925 p. 217.

11 *Ibid*.

12 C. E. M. Joad, *South Place Monthly Review*, May 1940, p. 5.

13 H. N. Brailsford, 'The Life-Work of J. A. Hobson', *L. T. Hobhouse Memorial*

Trust Lecture No. 17, Oxford, Oxford University Press, 1948, p. 4.

14 See, e.g., M. Bentley, *The Climax of Liberal Politics*, London, Arnold, 1987, p. 137.

15 *Derbyshire Advertiser,* 9 November 1893.

16 *Ibid.,* 9 October 1891; cf. *Ibid.,* 23 April 1893; and *CEH* p. 18.

17 *Derbyshire Advertiser*, 31 October 1890

18 *Ibid.,* 8 July 1893

19 *Annual Register*, August 1891, p. 164.

20 P. Weiler, *The New Liberalism: Liberal Social Theory in Great Britain, 1889-1914*, New York, Garland Publishing, 1982, p. 61.

21 P. xxvi.

22 *Derbyshire Advertiser*, 22 May 1896.

23 *Ibid.,* 3 November 1893. See G. L. Bernstein, *Liberalism and Liberal Politics in Edwardian England*, London, Allen and Unwin, 1986, pp. 13-14.

24 *Derbyshire Advertiser*, 4 October 1895.

25 *Ibid.,* 8 May 1896.

26 'Introductory', Progressive Review, (1), 1896, p. 4; cf. P. F. Clarke, *Liberals and Social Democrats*, Cambridge, Cambridge University Press, 1978, p. 57.

27 Indeed, neither was Bentham. He held that the state should intervene on questions of old age pensions, a minimum wage, sickness benefits and education, securing an 'artificial identification' of interest.

28 Quoted W. Harrison, *Conflict and Compromise*, London, Collier-Macmillan, 1965, p. 105.

29 Quoted A. Bullock and M. Shock, *The Liberal Tradition, from Fox to Keynes*, London, Oxford University Press, p. xxvi.

30 Quoted F. W. Hirst, *Free Trade and the Manchester School*, 1903, p xii.

31 J. S. Mill, *Principles of Political Economy*, 11, fifth edn, London, Longmans, 1862, p. 572.

32 *On Liberty*, edited by D. Spitz, New York, Norton, 1975, p. 11.

33 J. S. Mill, *Representative Government*, London, Dent, 1910 edn, p. 195

34 *Ibid.*, pp. 347-8.

35 *Ibid.*, p. 235.

36 Although he was not clear as to what precisely constituted the common good. See M. Freeden, *The New Liberalism: an Ideology of Social Reform*, Oxford, Clarendon Press, 1978, p. 57.

37 A. Vincent and R. Plant, *Philosophy, Politics and Citizenship*, Oxford, Blackwell, 1984, *passim*; M. Richter, *The Politics of Conscience: T. H. Green and his Age*, London, Weidenfeld and Nicolson, pp. 341-2.

38 This may also have had something to do with the neo-Hegelian atmosphere

of the London Ethical Society, which was run by disciples of T. H. Green, J. H. Muirhead and Bernard Bosanquet.

39 See J. Allett, *New Liberalism: the Political Economy of J. A. Hobson*, Toronto, University of Toronto Press, 1981, p. 19; M. Freeden, 'Biological and evolutionary roots of the new liberalism in England', *Political Theory*, 4, (4), (November 1976), p. 480.

Chapter 2

1 Although he was inconsistent in his definition of socialism – see Chapter 7 – he usually identified it as the state control of production, distribution and exchange.

2 See e.g., *The Crisis of Liberalism*, London, King, 1909, p. 116 (*CL* hereafter).

3 H. N. Brailsford, 'The Life-Work of J. A. Hobson', *L. T. Hobhouse Memorial Trust Lecture*, No 17, Oxford, Oxford University Press, 1948, p. 5.

4 *Confessions of an Economic Heretic* (*CEH* hereafter) p. 37.

5 *Work and Wealth: a Human Evaluation*, London, Macmillan, 1914, p. 17 (*WW* hereafter).

6 *CL*, p. xi [emphasis added].

7 *South Place Magazine*, 9, January 1904, p. 49; Cf. *Wealth and Life*, London, Macmillan, 1929, p. 17 (*WL* hereafter), *CL*, p. 273.

8 *WW* , p. 350.

9 *WL*, p. 14; cf. p. 62, pp. 321-2.

10 *WL*, p. 15.

11 *Evolution of Modern Capitalism*, London, Scott, 1894, p. 370 (*EMC* hereafter).

12 *WL*, p. 50.

13 *EMC,* p. 377.

14 E.g. *CL*, p. 262.

15 *WL*, p. 135.

16 Cf. *Free Thought in the Social Sciences*, London, Allen and Unwin, 1926, p. 144. (*FTSS* hereafter).

17 *WW*, p. 23.

18 *FTSS*, p. 171; *WL* pp. 72-3.

19 *The Industrial System*, London, Longmans, 1909, first edn, p. 317 (*IS* hereafter).

20 *CEH*, p. 56.

21 *WL*, p. 16.

22 E.g. *The Social Problem*, London, Nisbet, 1901, p. vi (*SP* hereafter); *WL*, p. 16; *FTSS*, pp. 167-73; cf. *WW* chs 3 and 12, *passim*.

23 *SP*, p. 82.

24 'The Wholeness of Life', *Ethical World*, 2, 28 April 1899, p. 216.
25 *WL*, p. 11.
26 *WL*, p. 13.
27 *WL*, p. 51, cf. p. xxv.
28 *WL*, p. 14.
29 *WL*, p. 13.
30 *WL*, p. 72.
31 *WL*, p. 20.
32 *EMC*, p. 365.
33 *WW*, p. 308.
34 *CEH*, p. 77.
35 *WW*, p. 307, 308.
36 *WW*, pp. 350-1.
37 Hobson's emphasis, *WW*, p. 308.
38 *WW*, p. 308; cf. *WL*, pp. 27-8; *CL* p. 73.
39 *WW*, p. 16.
40 *WW*, p. 356
41 *WW*, p. 355
42 *WW*, p. 26; cf. *CL*, p. 189.
43 *WW*, p. 357.
44 *CL*, p. 83.
45 *CL*, p. 78; cf. *WL*, pp. 42-3; *Democracy in a Changing Civilisation*, London, John Lane, 1934, p. 82 (*DCC* hereafter).
46 *CEH*, p. 14.
47 *EMC*, p. 365.
48 *Ibid.*
49 *EMC*, p. 377.
50 *EMC*, pp. 358-9.
51 *SP*, p.147; cf. *Taxation in the New State*, London, Methuen, pp. 70-1.
52 *SP*, p. 147; *WL*, p. 27.
53 *Evidence to the Committee on the National Debt and Taxation*, 1 (1924) p. 119; *Poverty in Plenty*, pp. 40-1, 1931, 'The Modern State', *Changing World*, 4 (1931), p. 19.
54 *SP*, pp. 150-2, *WW*, p. 305.
55 *WW*, p. 304.
56 *SP*, p. 224.
57 *CL*, p. 81.
58 *CL*, p. 86.
59 'After the Destruction of the Veto', *English Review*, 4, (1909), p. 117.

60 *CL*, p. 86.
61 *WL*, p. 389.
62 *SP*, p. 153; cf. WL, p. 167.
63 *WW*, p. 298.
64 *Ibid.*
65 *SP*, p. 225.
66 *SP*, p. 223.
67 *Ibid.*
68 *SP*, p. 225.
69 *SP*, 261.
70 *Ibid.*
71 *WW*, p. 360.
72 *WW*, p. 340.
73 *WW*, p. 341; cf. *WL*, pp. 66-7.
74 *WW*, p. 341.
75 *FTSS*, p. 65.
76 *WW*, p. 1.
77 *SP*, p. 1.
78 *CL*, p. 275.
79 *Problem of the Unemployed*, London, Methuen, 1896, third edn, 1906, p. viii.
80 *SP*, p. 234.
81 *SP*, pp. 66-7.
82 *SP*, p. 65; cf. *SP*, pp. 281-2; WL, p. 6.
83 *WL*, p. 125, (Hobson's emphasis)
84 See *SP*, p. 63, *WL*, p. 135.
85 *SP*, p. 57, *WL*, pp. 136-7.
86 *SP*, p. 56; cf. *WW*, p. 167; *CEH*, p. 170.
87 *International Journal of Ethics*, 25 (1915), pp. 265-8.

Chapter 3

1 *CEH*, p. 38; G. D. H. Cole, 'J. A. Hobson', *New Statesman*, 56, July 1958, p. 12.
2 *CEH*, p. 42.
3 *WL*, p. xxi.
4 John Ruskin, London, Nisbet, 1898, p. 80 (*JR* hereafter).
5 *JR*, p. 89.
6 *SP*, p. 118, emphasis in original. Hobson, in order to give this injunction a naturalistic underpinning, substituted 'can' for 'shall'.
7 'Ruskin and Democracy', *Contemporary Review*, January 1902, pp. 103-13; cf.

JR, p. 192.

8 WW, p. 10; *CEH*, p. 41.

9 *JR*, p. 101.

10 *SP*, pp. 48-9; cf. *JR*, pp. 101-2.

11 *SP*, p. 19.

12 *WL*, p. 108.

13 *SP*, p. 39.

14 *WL*, p. 109.

15 *SP*, p. 28.

16 SP, p. 18.

17 *The Economics of Distribution*, New York, Macmillan, 1900, pp. 219-22 (*ED* hereafter); cf.*WL*, pp. 208-9.

18 *FTSS*, pp. 71-2; cf. *SP*, pp. 22-3.

19 *SP*, pp. 26-7, *FTSS*, pp. 83-4.

20 *FTSS*, p. 75.

21 *SP*, p. 30; *FTSS*, p. 75.

22 *SP*, pp. 30-1.

23 *SP*, pp. 33-4.

24 *FTSS*, p. 106.

25 *SP*, p. 37.

26 *SP*, pp. 37-8.

27 *FTSS*, p. 93; cf. *WL*, p. 103.

28 *FTSS*, p. 97.

29 *FTSS*, pp. 97-101; *WW*, p. 32; cf. *WL*, pp. 103-4.

30 *FTSS*, p. 111.

31 *FTSS*, p. 109; cf. *Property and Improperty*, London, Gollancz, 1937, p. 217 (*P and I* hereafter).

32 *FTSS*, p. 115.

33 *Ibid.*, p. 115).

34 *Ibid.*, p.117.

35 *Ibid.*, p. 120.

36 *Ibid.*, p. 122.

37 *Ibid.*, p. 121, cf. *P and I*, p. 221.

38 *FTSS*, p. 122.

39 *WW*, p. 334; cf. *WL*. p. 110).

40 *WL*, p. 108.

41 *WL*, p. 109.

42 *WL*, p. 111.

43 *WW*, p. 360.

44 *WW,* p. 321; cf. *SP,* p. 287.

45 *WW,* p. 322;; cf. *WL,* pp. v-vi, 51, 53, 63-4, *FTSS,* p. 142.

46 *WL,* p. 59.

47 *Ibid.*

48 *WL,* p. 60; cf. *SP,* p. 87; *FTSS,* p. 144.

49 *WL,* p. 60.

50 *Ibid.*

51 *WL,* p. 63.

52 *SP,* p. ,vi; *WL,* p. 16; *FTSS,* pp. 167-73.

53 *WW,* p. 161.

54 *Ibid.*

55 *Ibid.*

56 *WW,* p. 36.

57 *WW,* p. 320; cf. *FTSS,* p. 143.

58 *WW,* p. 321; cf. *FTSS,* p. 142; *WL,* p. 58.

59 *WW,* p. 44; *SP,* p. 46.

60 *WW,* p. 62.

61 *WW,* p. 63.

62 *WW,* Ch. 6 *passim.*

63 *WW,* p. 79.

64 *WW,* p. 101.

65 *WW,* p. 104.

66 *WW,* p. 107; cf. *SP,* p. 48.

67 *WW,* p. 108; cf. *SP,* p. 49.

68 *WW,* p. 122.

69 *WW,* p. 121.

70 S. Hook, *From Hegel to Marx,* Michigan, University of Michigan Press, 1950, 1962 edn, pp. 267-71.

71 *WW,* p. 124.

72 *WW,* p. 125.

73 Whether this was a retrospective criticism of his own athletic prowess as a high jumper we shall not know.

74 *WW,* p. 150. cf. *SP,* pp. 78-84.

75 *WW,* p. 151. Again, personal experience? His undergraduate studies in Classics at Oxford?

76 *WW,* p. 152.

77 J. Allett, *New Liberalism: the Political Economy of J. A. Hobson,* Toronto, University of Toronto Press, 1981, p. 255.

78 *Ibid.,* p. 75.

79 *SP*, p. 147. Hobson could easily have derived this idea from Marx's *Capital*, 1, which we know that he had read (see *EMC*, first edn, 1894, pp. 45-6). Marx refers to the 'social productive power of the combined working day' which was 'due to co-operation itself' (*Capital*, Harmondsworth, Penguin, 1976, vol. 1, p. 329.

80 *Ibid.*

81 Allett, *New Liberalism*, p. 77.

82 *Ibid.*, p. 76.

83 *SP*, p. 148.

84 *IS*, second edn, p. 136.

85 *Ibid.*, p. xii. Allett (pp. 76-7) unfortunately quotes a passage from *IS* , second edn, p. 136 to demonstrate the social character of the surplus, when Hobson is clearly referring to an 'industrial surplus' rather than an 'organic surplus'.

86 E.g. *IS,* second edn, p. 79, p. 331, *Conditions of Industrial Peace*, London, Allen and Unwin, p. 21, p. 119

87 He also called it 'unearned' surplus, or later 'improperty', *Democracy after the War*, London, Allen and Unwin, fourth edn, 1919, p. 51 (*DAW* hereafter).

88 *IS*, p. xi.

89 *WW*, p. vii. cf. *IS*, p. 78.

90 *WW*, p. 187; cf. *WL*, p. 199; *IS*, p. 331.

91 *WW*, p. 187.

92 *WL*, p. 200.

93 *Ibid.*

94 Hobson, 'Law of Three Rents', *Quarterly Journal of Economics*, 5 (1890-91), pp. 263-88; S. Webb, 'The Rate of Interest', and 'The Laws of Distribution', *Quarterly Journal of Economics,* 2, pp. 188-208, 469-72; cf. A. M. McBriar, *Fabian Socialism and English Politics, 1884-1918*, Cambridge, Cambridge University Press, p. 39; and D. M. Ricci, 'Fabian Socialism: a Theory of Rent as Exploitation', *Journal of British Studies*, 9 (1) (1969), pp. 105-21.

95 See, e.g. *CEH*, pp. 47-8.

96 *IS*, pp. 150-4; *WL*, pp. 203-4.

97 *ED*, p. 222.

98 See, e.g., 'Saving and Sending', n.d., 1923-4 ?

99 *WL*, p. 210.

110 In *P and I* p. 15 there seems to be a little volte-face on this question.

101 *FTSS*, p. 154; cf. 'A British Socialism', *New Statesman*, 2 (1936), p. 107.

102 *FTSS*, p. 48.

103 *FTSS*, p. 147.

104 'Thoughts on Our Present Discontents', *Political Quarterly,* 9 (1938), pp. 47-57; *FTSS*, p. 150.

105 *CEH*, p. 35.

106 Cf. *WL*, p. 78; *FTSS*, p. 29.

107 Hobson papers fragment pp. 12-13. Indeed, there are a number of similarities between Marx's and Hobson's theorising, e.g between 'individuation' and the overcoming of alienation, and the significance of the machine in this process, see Chapter 7.

108 *CEH,* p. 35.

109 *FTSS*, p. 153.

110 *FTSS*, p. 154.

111 *ED*, p. 63.

112 *ED*, p. 68.

113 *ED*, p. 354. cf. *DAW*, p. 32.

114 *CEH*, p. 168.

115 *The Physiology of Industry,* London, Murray, 1889, p. iv. cf. pp. 97-8 (*PI*, hereafter)

116 *IS*, p. 284.

117 *The Problem of the Unemployed,* London, Methuen, third edn, 1906, p. 88, 91.

118 *PU*, pp. 79-80.

119 *PU*, p. 46.

120 *IS*, p. 289.

121 *IS*, pp. 291-2.

122 *PI*, Ch. 7 *passim.*

123 *IS*, pp. 298-9; cf.*Economics of Unemployment*, London, Macmillan, 1922, pp. 62-3 (*EU* hereafter).

124 *WL*, pp. 291-2; cf. 'Underconsumption: an Exposition and Reply', *Economica*, 13 (1933), pp. 402-17.

125 *EU*, p. 122.

126 But also Barbara Wootton, see Allett, *New Liberalism,* p. 126.

127 Keynes, *General Theory*, pp. 367-70; cf. G. Foote, *The Labour Party's Political Thought*, London, Croom Helm, 1985, pp. 165-6.

128 P. Clarke, *Liberals and Social Democrats*, Cambridge, Cambridge University Press, 1978, pp. 271-2.

129 *CEH*, pp. 192-3n; Allett, *New Liberalism*, p. 128; See D. J. Coppock, in 'A Reconsideration of Hobson's Theory of Unemployment', *Manchester School of Economic and Social Studies*, 21 (1953), p. 21, who argues that Keynes and

Hobson's positions were much closer than they both realized.

130 Cf. Clarke, *Liberals and Social Democrats*, p. 230.

131 *JR*, p. 36.

132 *Poverty in Plenty*, London, Allen and Unwin, 1931.

Chapter 4

1 There was a good deal of terminological and conceptual slippage in his use of the term 'socialism', see final chapter.

2 *CEH*, p. 199.

3 E.g. *CEH*, pp. 125-6, *WL*, p. 235.

4 *Problems of Poverty*, London, Methuen, 1891, p. 174 (*PP* hereafter).

5 *PP*, pp. 171-82.

6 'The Social Philosophy of Charity Organisation', *Contemporary Review*, 70 (1896), pp. 710-27, later republished in *CL*, pp. 192-217.

7 *CL*, p. 207.

8 *Ibid.*, p. 216.

9 *Ibid.*, p. 196; *SP*, p. 113.

10 *CL*, pp. 215-16.

11 *Ibid.*, pp. 204-5.

12 *PP*, p. 175.

13 *Ibid.*, p. 175; cf. *FTSS*, p. 230; *CL*, p. 206.

14 *CL*, p. 217.

15 *Ibid.*, p. 173.

16 E.g. *CEH*, pp. 125-6; *WL*, p. 235. Indeed, there is a striking parallel between Hobson's defence of (limited) economic liberty, and J. S. Mill's justification of individual liberty on the grounds of its contribution to social progress. See *On Liberty*, pp. 66-9, edited by . D. Spitz, New York, Norton, 1975.

17 *FTSS*, pp. 135-6; cf. *P and I*, p. 29.

18 *WL*, pp. 232-3.

19 *CL*, p. 172.

20 *Ibid.*, pp. 172-3.

21 *IS*, p. 322.

22 *WW*, p. 178.

23 *CL*, p. 86.

24 *WW*, p. 169.

25 *IS*, p. 322.

26 *SP*, p. 152.

27 *WW*, pp. 163-4.

28 E.g. *IS*, p. 319.

29 *WW*, p. 298.

30 *CIP*, pp. 21, 118.

31 *IS*, p. 321; cf. *WL*, p. 208.

32 *IS*, p. 80.

33 Although he effectively came to realise that there were certain ethical deficiencies with this formula (*WL*, p. 208n).

34 *SP*, p. 162; cf. *WW*, p. 164.

35 *SP*, p. 164.

36 *Ibid.*, p. 165.

37 *IS*, pp. 320-1.

38 *Ibid.*, p. 319.

39 *Ibid.*

40 *IS*, pp. 320-1.

41 *SP*, p. 172; cf. *WW*, p. 170; *WL*, p. 438; *CEH*, p. 125.

42 *WL*, p. 438; cf. *WL*, p. 208n.

43 *SP*, p. 173.

44 Pp. 346-7, *The First International and After*, edited by. D. Fernbach, Harmondsworth, Penguin, 1974.

45 Why should an individual who is able to get the most satisfaction out of a given income necessarily be the same person who ought receive that income according to productivity or skill?

46 *WW*, p. 164; cf. *WL*, p. 316.

47 See, e.g., *WW*, p. 167; *WL*, p. 448.

48 *WW*, p. 168; cf. pp. 190-2.

49 *WW*, pp. 194-5.

50 *Ibid.*, p. 192.

51 *Ibid.*, pp. 168-9.

52 E.g., *SP*, pp. 170-1; *WW*, p. 169.

53 *IS*, p. 210.

54 *CL*, p. 174.

55 *WL*, pp. 42-4.

56 *WW*, p. 165.

57 *WL*, p. 443; cf. *SP*, p. 166.

58 *IS*, pp. 322-4.

59 E.g. *EMC*, pp. 381-3.

60 E.g. *IS*, p. 210.

61 *Ibid.*, p. 208.

62 E.g. *P and I*, p. 183.

63 *IS*, pp. 233-4; *WL*, p. 442.

64 *IS*, p. 215.

65 *WW*, p. 197; *IS*, p. 213, first edn.

66 *WL*, p. 200.

67 *CIP*, p. 105.

68 *CIP*, p. 30.

69 *Democracy in a Changing Civilisation,* London, Bodley Head, 1934, p. 118 (*DCC* hereafter).

70 *WW*, p. 82; cf. *SP*, p. 9.

71 *IS*, p. 214.

72 *Ibid.,* p. 213.

73 *Ibid.,* Ch. 17 *passim.*

74 *WW*, p. 234; *WL*, p. 259.

75 *WW*, p. 236.

76 *WW*, p. 236; cf. *SP*, pp. 11-12, 236; 'The ethics of industrialism', in *Ethical Democracy: Essays in Social Dynamics,* edited by. S. Coit, London, Grant Richards, 1900, p. 106.

77 *WW*, pp. 238-40.

78 *Ibid.,* pp. 248-9.

79 See, e.g., *P and I*, p. 179.

80 *SP*, p. 170; *WW*, p. 169; 'Ethics of industrialism', p. 98.

81 Pp. 96-113; cf. pp. 159-75.

82 *CL*, p. 109; cf. Pt 3, Ch. 1 *passim*

83 *IS*, p. 210.

84 See 'The Limits of Collectivism', *Contemporary Review*, 63 (1893), pp. 263-78, and even possibly H. D. Lloyd (see H. Pelling, *America and the British Left*, London, Black, 1956, p. 59; C. Lloyd, *Henry Demarest Lloyd*, New York, Putnams, 1912, 1, pp. 298-300; S. Fine, *Laissez-faire and the General Welfare State*, Ann Arbor, University of Michigan Press, 1956, p. 350). See also an account of the Fabians' general position on the question in McBriar, *Fabian Socialism and English Politics*, p. 111.

85 Although Brailsford, in 'The Life-Work of J. A. Hobson', p. 20, suggests that Hobson on occasion invoked other criteria in assessing which firms ought to be nationalised.

86 *EMC*, p. 371.

87 *Ibid.,* pp. 369-70.

88 *Ibid.,* p. 372.

89 Although he was uncertain about what form the regulation of land should take, given the importance of 'personal individual interest and activity' in agricultural production, *P and I*, p. 194.

90 *EMC*, pp. 382-3.

91 *Ibid.*, p. 371.

92 *SP*, p. 184.

93 *CEH*, p. 125.

94 See, e.g., *WL*, p. 438.

95 *P and I*, p. 188.

96 *Ibid.*, p. 197.

97 *Ibid.*, p. 195; *CEH*, pp. 171-2, *DCC*, pp. 104-7.

98 *EMC*, p. 364.

99 *WW*, p. 288.

100 *EMC*, p. 363.

101 *Ibid.*

102 *WL*, p. 385; cf. 'A British Socialism', *New Statesman*, 11, 25 January 1936, pp. 107-8. Allett, in *New Liberalism*, p. 249, following Brailsford, seems to assume that Hobson totally ignored the question of innovation and incentive in public enterprises

103 *WL*, pp. 269-70, 287-8; cf. *DCC*, pp. 104-7; 'Is Socialism Tyranny?', *Nation*, 2, 26 October 1907, p. 119.

104 *Problems of a New World*, London, Allen and Unwin, 1921, p. 241 (*PNW* hereafter), *WL*, pp. 388-9.

105 *SP*, p. 288.

106 E.g. *CL*, p. 35; *DAW*, p. 152.

107 *I*, pp. 145-9.

108 *DAW*, pp. 152-3.

109 *CL*, p. 16; *Towards International Government*, London, Macmillan, 1915, p. 207 (*TIG* hereafter); cf. *FTSS*, p. 231 and Allett 216-22.

110 *WL*, p. 266.

111 See *CL*, p. 9 and *TIG*, p. 186, 201-2 for detailed proposals.

112 *DCC*, p. 102; cf. *CL*, p. 47.

113 'After the Destruction of the Veto', *English Review*, 4 (1909), p. 117.

114 *CL*, p. 41.

115 *DCC*, p. 102.

116 *CL*, pp. 86-7.

117 *SP*, p. 240.

118 *DCC*, pp. 108-10.

119 E.g. *I*, pp. 188-9.

120 *FTSS*, pp. 216-17.

121 *SP*, p. 217.

122 *WW*, p. 318.

123 *WL*, p. 359; cf. *CEH*, p. 152.
124 *WL*, pp. 363-4.
125 E.g. *WW*, p. 242; *WL*, p. xxx.

Chapter 5

1 This chapter based upon my introduction to a re-issue of Hobson's *Imperialism*, London, Unwin Hyman, 1988.
2 *Imperialism: a Study, London*, Allen and Unwin, third edn, 1938, p. 246, first edn, 1902 (*I* hereafter).
3 I, p. 23.
4 *Ibid.*, p. 246.
5 *Ibid.*, pp. 11, 55, 65, 200.
6 *Ibid.*, p. 8, p. 304.
7 *Ibid.*, p. 304.
8 *Ibid.*, p. 6, p. 37, p. 124.
9 *Ibid.*, p. 7.
10 We should note that most of these arguments were formulated originally by Adam Smith, Jeremy Bentham and James Mill, but Cobden popularised them.
11 *I*, p. 152.
12 *Ibid.*, p. 133.
13 *Ibid.*, p. 150.
14 *Ibid.*, pp. 145-8.
15 See P. Cain, 'J. A. Hobson, Cobdenism, and the Radical Theory of Economic Imperialism, 1898-1914', *Economic History Review*, second series, 31 (1978), p. 568.
16 Cobden, *Political Writings*, London, Cassell, 1886, pp. 24, 36-8; Hobson, *I*, pp. 68-9, 362.
17 *I*, pp. 28-31, a point well made in Peter Cain's article 'J. A Hobson, Cobdenism, and the Radical Theory of Economic Imperialism, 1898-1914'. See also Townshend, introduction to *Imperialism*, 1988, p. 382, for changes made in subsequent editions to *Imperialism*.
18 *I*, p. 367.
19 Hobson, *SP*, p. 118, original emphasis.
20 *I*, p. 243.
21 *Ibid.*, p. 246.
22 *Ibid.*, pp. 246-84.
23 *Ibid.*, p. 285.

24 *Ibid.*, p. 324.

25 *Ibid.*, p. 55.

26 *Ibid.*, p. 50.

27 See e.g., W. L. Langer, *The Diplomacy of Imperialism*, New York, Knopf, 1935, 1, p. 74.

28 *I*, pp. 264-6.

29 Hobson, *The Psychology of Jingoism*, London, Richards, 1901 (*PJ* hereafter).

30 *PJ*, pp. 6-7.

31 *PJ*, pp. 9-10, *I*, pp. 213-15.

32 *Ibid.*, pp. 197-8.

33 *Ibid.*, p. 246.

34 *Ibid.*, p. 216.

35 *Ibid.*, p. 363.

36 *Ibid.*, pp. 88-91.

37 *Ibid.*, p. 188.

38 *Ibid.*, pp. 190-1.

39 *Ibid.*, p. 225.

40 *I*, pp 226-7; cf. *WL*, pp. 394-6. Indeed, this argument goes back at least as far as John Locke, who had insisted that the earth had been given to the 'industrious and rational', *The Second Treatise of Government,* edited by P. Laslett, Cambridge, Cambridge University Press, 1988, p. 291.

41 *I*, p. 255.

42 *Ibid.*, p. 230.

43 *Ibid.*, p. 231.

44 *Ibid.*, p. 229. See J. Townshend, 'J. A. Hobson: Anti-Imperialist?' *International Review of History and Political Science*, 19 (3), August 1982, pp. 28-41 for a discussion of Hobson's imperialistic tendencies.

45 *I*, p. 185.

46 *SP*, p. 276; B. Porter, *Critics of Empire*, London, Macmillan, 1968, p. 182.

47 *Towards International Government*, London, Macmillan, 1915, pp. 137-42 (*TIG* hereafter).

48 *TIG*, chs 3 and 4 *passim*; *WL*, p. 393.

49 'Capitalism and Imperialism in South Africa', *Contemporary Review*, 77 (1990), p. 15.

50 *CEH*, p. 63.

51 Porter, *Critics of Empire*, p. 222.

52 *FTSS*, p. 192; *I*, p. v.

53 *I*, p. 190; Cain, 'J. A. Hobson, Cobdenism, and the Radical Theory of Imperialism, 1898-1914'.

54 'Hobson's Developing Theory of Imperialism', *Economic History Review*, second series, 34, (1981), p. 315. Peter Clarke, in a critique of Cain's interpretation, suggests that Hobson's 'basic conceptions and values' were more constant over time, if not at any particular time. ('Hobson, Free Trade and Imperialism', *Economic History Review*, second series, 34 (1981), p. 308. It should be fairly self-evident that the perspective offered here is strongly at variance with Clarke's.

55 *I*, p. 229; cf. *SP*, p. 174.

56 *An Economic Interpretation of Investment,* London, Financial Review of Reviews, 1911, p. 19 (*EII* hereafter).

57 K. Kautsky, 'Ultra Imperialism', *New Left Review*, 59 (1970), pp. 39-46.

58 *I*, p. 311.

59 *EII*, p. 113; cf. *Science of Wealth,* London, Home University Library, 1911, p. 242 (*SW* hereafter); cf. *WW* p. 274.

60 *I*, p. 59, pp. 130-1

61 *Ibid*., pp. 55-6.

62 *Ibid*., p. 55, pp. 95-6.

63 'Why the War Came as a Surprise', *Political Science Quarterly*, 35 (1920), p. 337.

64 *DAW*, p. 27.

65 *I*, p. xxii.

66 *I*, pp. v-vi.

67 'The Life-Work of J. A. Hobson', p. 26.

68 *DCC*, pp. 135, 152.

69 *CEH*, p. 113.

70 See D. K. Fieldhouse (ed), *The Theory of Capitalist Imperialism*, London, Longman, 1967, *passim*.

Chapter 6

1 *CEH*, p. 56.

2 See e.g., 'The Significance of the Budget', *The English Review*, 2, July 1909, p. 794.

3 *FTSS*, p. 249.

4 *CEH*, p. 57.

5 *DAW*, 1917 edn, p. 139; cf. *PNW* , p. 208.

6 Lloyd George made similar remarks in 1906. See W. S. Adams, 'Lloyd George and the Labour Movement', *Past and Present*, 3 (1953), p. 59.

7 'Economics for a People's Front', *Labour Monthly*, 19, January 1937, p. 21.

8 Hobson to O. G. Villard, 15 October 1927, quoted Clarke, *Liberals and Social*

Democrats, pp. 241-2.

9   *CEH*, p. 168; cf. *The Living Wage* (with H. N. Brailsford, A. Creech Jones, E. F. Wise), London, Independent Labour Party, p. 54.

10 *PNW*, pp. 211-12.

11 *DAW*, p. 139; cf. *WL*, pp.xxviii-xxix, *Poverty in Plenty*, London, Allen and Unwin, 1931, p. 46.

12 *Poverty in Plenty*, p. 83.

13 *Ibid.*

14 *God and Mammon*, London, Watts, 1931, p. 50.

15 *SP*, pp.1-2, 257-8; *DAW*, 4th edn, 1919, pp. 152-3; cf. 'Introductory', *Progressive Review*, 1896. p. 3.

16 Clarke, *Liberals and Social Democrats*, p. 58.

17 E.g. 'Introductory', p. 3.

18 *DA*, 13 March, 1896.

19 *DA*, 4 January, 1895.

20 *DA*, 8 May, 1896.

21 *DA*, 22 May, 1896.

22 Cf. D. Marquand, *Ramsay MacDonald*, London, Cape, 1977, p. 56.

23 'Free Trade and Foreign Policy', *Contemporary Review*, 74 1898), p. 167.

24 'Is the Future with Socialism ?', *Ethical World*, 2, 18 March 1899, pp. 168-9.

25 Quoted Allett, *New Liberalism*, p. 23; Samuel Papers, File A 10 August 1894.

26 *DA*, 24 November, 1896.

27 *CEH*, p. 54.

28 H. Samuel, *Memoirs,* London, Cresset Press, 1945, p. 24; Clarke, *Liberals and Social Democrats*, p. 60.

29 Stapley papers i, p. 87.

30 *Ibid.*

31 H. Pelling, *Origins of the Labour Party*, London, Oxford University Press, second edn, 1965, p. 189.

32 *New Age*, 9 January,.1901.

33 *I*, p. 143.

34 *Ibid.*, pp. 101-2.

35 *South Place Magazine*, March 1901, pp. 91-2.

36 *I*, pp. 144-5.

37 'The Soul of Illiberalism', *New Age*, 11 July, 1901.

38 Quoted Pelling, *Origins of the Labour Party*, pp. 226-7.

39 'The Crisis of Trade Unionism', *New Age*, 26 September,1907 .

40 *Ibid.* 'Le Socialisme Sans Doctrines' was the title of a book written by a

Belgian writer, A. Metin, on the Australian Labor Party.

41 15 October, 1901.

42 *Ibid.*

43 *Ibid.*

44 *Ibid.*

45 Echo, 16 October, 17 October, 19 October.

46 See, J. K. Hardy and J. R. MacDonald, 'The Liberal Collapse', The Nineteenth Century, 45 (1899), p. 27 for earlier ILP offer to co-operate with Liberals over specific issues.

47 *Echo*, 17 October 1901.

48 *Labour Leader*, 19 October 1901.

49 *Ibid.*, 26 October 1901.

50 *Ibid.*, 26 October 1901.

51 *Ibid.*

52 H. Pelling, *Origins of the Labour Party*, p. 227.

53 *Labour Leader*, 30 November 1901.

54 *Tribune*, 15 January 1906, 12 Febuary,1906.

55 *CEH*, p. 83; cf. B. Gilbert, *The Evolution of National Insurance in Great Britain*, London, 1966, Joseph, p. 69.

56 Here, I strongly depart from Cain's assertion that in the decade before 1914 Hobson believed 'in the coming of the New Jerusalem' as a result of the Liberal's coming to power. 'J. A Hobson, Cobdenism, and the Radical Theory of Economic Imperialism, 1898-1914', p. 565.

57 Nation, 2, 12 October1907, pp. 37-8 later reprinted in *CL*, p. 133.

58 *CL*, p. xii.

59 *Ibid.*

60 'The Significance of the Budget', *English Review*, 2, July 1901, p. 801.

61 *Manchester Guardian*, 13 March 1908.

62 *CL*, pp. 91-2.

63 *CL*, p. 135.

64 *Ibid.*

65 *Ibid.*

66 *Ibid.*

67 *CL*, pp. 135-6.

68 *CL*, p. 136.

69 P. Weiler, *The New Liberalism: Liberal Social Theory in Great Britain, 1889-1914*, New York, Garland, 1982, p. 109.

70 *Traffic in Treason: a Study in Political Parties*, London, T. Fisher Unwin, 1914, p. 61 (*TT* hereafter).

71 *Ibid.*

72 *TT*, p. 63.

73 Quoted T. Wilson, *The Political Diaries of C. P. Scott, 1911-1928*, London, Collins, 1970, pp. 87-8

74 Quoted A. J. Lee, 'The Social and Political Thought of J. A. Hobson', unpublished Ph.D. thesis, University of London, 1970, p. 533.

75 *Nation*, 12, 26 June 1912, p. 464.

76 Quoted A. J. A. Morris, 'The English Radicals' Campaign for Disarmament and the Hague Conference of 1907', *Journal of Modern History*, 43 (1971), pp. 367-93.

77 *Nation*, 19, 10 June 1916, p. 308.

78 M. Swartz, *The U.D.C. in British Politics During the First World War*, Oxford, Clarendon, 1971, p. 86; R. E. Dowse, 'The Entry of the Liberals into the Labour Party, 1910-1920', *Yorkshire Bulletin of Economic and Social Research*, 13 (1961-62), pp. 78-88; G. P. Gooch, *Under Six Reigns*, London, Longmans, 1958, p. 77.

79 Cf. P. Clarke, *Liberals and Social Democrats*, p. 195; C. A. Cline, *Recruits to Labour*, New York, Syracuse University Press, 1963, p. 17.

80 M. Swartz, *The U.D.C. in British Politics During the First World War*, p. 212.

81 C. P. Scott, *Diaries*, 50907/116. 16 July 1924.

82 *CEH*, p. 126.

83 *CEH*, p. 121; *WL*, p. 172; *EMC*, 1926 edn, p. 485; *South Place Magazine*, 2 June,1912.

84 *EMC*, 1926 edn. p. 485.

85 *CEH*, p. 121.

86 See Skidelsky, *Politicians and the Slump 1929-31*, London, Macmillan, 1967, p. 66,

87 C.P. Scott, *Diaries* 50907/116, 16 July 1924.

88 Nation, New York, 11 November 1925, pp. 542-3.

89 New Leader, 15 January 1926, p. 4.

90 *Nation*, New York, 126, 20 June 1928, p. 689.

91 *Nation*, 128, 15 May 1929, p. 582; cf. *Manchester Guardian*, 9 Febuary 1929.

Chapter 7

1 M. Freeden, (ed.), *J. A. Hobson: a Reader*, London, Unwin Hyman, 1988, p. 22.

2 Freeden, in *The New Liberalism*, Oxford, Clarendon Press, 1986, p. 5, does not quite say this although he comes close to it, and moreover his continual references to Hobson as a 'liberal' gives the impression that Hobson was

theoretically a liberal.

3 *SP*, p. 154.

4 *CL*, p. 172.

5 E.g. *CL*, p. 172.

6 *CL*, p. xii.

7 *CL*, p. 172.

8 'Is the Future with Socialism ?' *Ethical World*, 2, 18 March 1899, p 168; cf. 'Kidd's Social Evolution', *American Journal of Sociology*, 1 (1895), p. 307.

9 *P and I*, pp. 179-80.

10 'The Fourfold Path of Socialism', *Nation*, 2, 30 November 1907, p.303.

11 M. Freeden, *J. A. Hobson: a Reader*, p. 190; cf. Clarke, *Liberals and Social Democrats*, p. 182.

12 'The Claims of the State upon the Individual', *Nation*, 19, 10 June 1916, pp. 307-8; Freeden, *J. A. Hobson. a Reader*, p. 197, quoted Clarke, *Liberals and Social Democrats*, p. 82.

13 *WL*, pp. 35-6.

14 E.g. 'Liberty as a True War Economy', *Nation*, 19, 29 July 1916, pp. 524-5.

15 E.g. *CL*, pp. 15-16.

16 Cf. Allett, *New Liberalism*, pp. 214-15, 258.

17 *The Conditions of Industrial Peace,* London, Allen and Unwin, 1927, pp. 120-1. (*CIP* hereafter); 'Democracy, Liberty and Force', *Hibbert Journal*, 33 (1935), p. 40.

18 *New Liberalism*, p. 180.

19 *WL*, p. 35.

20 T. W. Hutchinson, *A Review of Economic Doctrines, 1870-1929*, Oxford, Clarendon Press, 1966, p. 129.

21 *Manchester Guardian*, 2 April 1940.

22 See, e.g. J. K. Hardie and J. R. MacDonald, 'The Liberal Collapse', *The Nineteenth Century*, p. 26.

23 M. Freeden, *Liberalism Divided*, Oxford, Clarendon Press, 1986, ch. 8 *passim*.

24 M. G. Foote, *The Labour Party's Political Thought*, London, Croom Helm, 1985, pp. 56-64; R. Barker (ed.), *Ramsay MacDonald's Political Writings*, London, Allen Lane, 1972, p. 38.

24 This, one suspects, to be a little cynical, may have been in order to give greater legitimacy for his own ideas in the labour movement.

26 Foote, *The Labour Party's Political Thought*, p. 163.

27 Elizabeth Durbin, *New Jerusalems*, London, Routledge and Kegan Paul, 1985, ch. 7 *passim*.

28 'J. A. Hobson', *New Statesman*, 56 (1958), p.12.

29 A. W. Wright, *G, D. H. Cole and Socialist Democracy*, London, Oxford University Press, 186; Foote, *The Labour Party's Political Thought*, p. 185.

30 J. Dorfman, *The Economic Mind in American Civilzation*, New York, Viking, 1959, 5, pp. 588-9.

31 J. Allett, *New Liberalism*, p. 45.

32 *Ibid.*

33 P. T. Homan, *Contemporary Economic Thought,* New York, Harper, 1928.

34 See, I, 1988 edn., p. 383, note 32.

35 N. Etherington, *Theories of Imperialism*, London, Croom Helm, 1984, p. 189.

36 E. M. Winslow, *The Pattern of Imperialism*, New York, Columbia University Press, 1948, pp. 49-50.

37 H. Pelling, *America and the British Left*, pp. 59-60.

38 C. Lloyd, *Henry Demarest Lloyd*, pp. 298-300.

39 N. Etherington, *Theoroes of Imperialism*, ch. 3 *passim*. Etherington's claims for Wilshire's influence on Hobson are however somewhat exaggerated.

40 P. A. Baran and P. M. Sweezy, *Monopoly Capital*, Harmondsworth, Penguin, 1966, *passim*; A. Brewer, *Marxist Theories of Imperialism*, London, Routledge and Kegan Paul, 1980, p. 133.

41 F. M. Leventhal, *The Last Dissenter. H. N. Brailsford and His World*, Oxford, Clarendon Press, 1985, p. 109.

42 Foote, *The Labour Party's Political Thought*, p. 67.

43 A. J. P. Taylor, *The Trouble Makers*, London, Hamish Hamilton, 1957, p. 111.

44 J. Strachey, *The End of Empire*, London, Gollancz, 1959, pp, 112, 137.

45 R. Koebner, 'The Concept of Economic Imperialism', *Economic History Review,* second series, 2 (1949), pp. 3-4.

46 *New Liberalism*, p.24.

47 *Ibid.*, p. 253.

48 *Ibid.*, p. 100.

49 *Ibid.*, p.51.

50 *I*, p. 36.

51 *SP*, p. 118; cf. *WW*, p. 296, p. 351.

52 *SP*, p. 120.

53 E.g. *IS*, p. 80.

54 Cf. Hutchinson, *A Review of Economic Doctrines, 1870-1929*, p. 122; M. F. Bleaney, *Underconsumptionist Theories*, London, Lawrence and Wishart, 1976, p. 180.

55 This point is well made by Allett, *New Liberalism*, pp. 108-9.

56 Cf. Freeden, *New Liberalism*, p. 102 and *FTSS*, pp. 144-5.

57 *CEH*, pp. 42-3.

58 Allett, *New Liberalism*, p. 68.

59 *Ibid.*, p. 254.

60 *Ibid.*, p. 253.

61 Weiler, *The New Liberalism*, p. 169 and p. 175, suggests that this was his central difficulty, but does not pursue this line of analysis.

62 Cf. C. B. MacPherson, *Democratic Theory: Essays in Retrieval*, Oxford, Clarendon Press, 1973, Ch. 1, *passim*.

63 MacPherson, *Democratic Theory*, pp. 175-6.

64 *CL*, pp. 172-3.

65 *IS*, p. xii.

66 *SP*, p. 228.

67 E.g. *WW*, p. 168; *WL*, p. 435, although of course at the macro-level this might not be the case if an underconsumptionist model is used.

68 *WL*, p. 435; cf. *SP*, p. 107.

69 *WW*, p. 236.

70 *SP*, p. 11; *P and I*, p. 98.

71 *WL*, p. 233.

72 *WW*, pp. 306, 56. The two chapters in which these statements appear were among those that were cut from the revised 1933 edition of *WW*. Later, he retreated from this position, which he acknowledged as 'purely fanciful'. *WL*, p. 440.

73 E.g. *SP*, p. 162; *WW*, p. 164.

74 *SP*, p. 165.

75 *Ibid.*

76 *P and I*, p. 98; cf. *SP*, pp. 120-1.

77 *CEH*, p. 168.

78 *Ibid.*, p. 168. Cf. 'Ethics of Industrialism,' in S. Coit (ed.), *Ethical Democracy*, pp. 92 , 94; *WL*, p.206.

79 *CEH,* p. 168.

80 *CIP*, p. 73; cf. *Incentives in the New Industrial Order,* London, Parsons, 1922, p. 37 (*INIO* hereafter); *WW*, p. 253; *WL*, pp. 70, 190.

81 *CIP*, p. 119. Cf. IS, first edn, 1909, pp. 78-9.

82 *CIP*, p. 78.

83 *CIP*, p. 21.

84 *Ibid.*

85 'Ethics of Industrialism', p. 92.

86 *INIO*, p. 32.

87 E.g. *WL*, p. 271.

88 L. M. Mead, *Beyond Entitlement*, New York, Free Press, 1985; C. Murray, *Losing Ground*, New York, Basic Books, 1986.

89 E.g. D. Marquand, *The Unprincipled Society*, London, Cape, 1988, and R. Hattersley, *Choose Freedom*, Harmondsworth, Penguin, 1987.

90 The Affinities of Norbetto Bobbio', *New Left Review*, 170, July/August 1988, p. 5, n. 9.

91 *Farewell to the Working Class*, London, Pluto Press, 1982, ch. 8 *passim*.

Further reading

By Hobson

Someone coming fresh to Hobson can read a useful anthology of extracts from his works, edited by Michael Freeden, *J. A. Hobson: a Reader*, London, Unwin Hyman, 1988. A good overview of his social, political and economic theory is to be found in Hobson's *Confessions of an Economic Heretic*, edited by M. Freeden, Brighton, Harvester Press, 1976. On the more specific elements of his thought, the simplest introduction to his organic perspective is chapter 14 of the *Evolution of Modern Capitalism*, London, Scott, 1894. More detailed treatments are in *Work and Wealth*, London, Macmillan, 1914; and *Wealth and Life*, London, Macmillan, 1929. Indeed, these two works, along with *The Social Problem*, London, Nisbet, 1901, also give the best accounts of socio-economic philosophy, of his attempts to 'humanise' economics. His best critique of conventional economics is *Free Thought in the Social Sciences*, London, Allen and Unwin, 1926. His own 'positive' analysis of capitalism can be seen in a number of works. The most comprehensive is *The Industrial System*, London, Longmans, 1909, and a simplified version is *The Science of Wealth*, London, Williams and Northgate, 1911. The most detailed account, and defence, of his underconsumptionism is *The Economics of Unemployment*, London, Allen and Unwin, 1922. On political questions, *The Crisis of Liberalism*, Brighton, Harvester Press, 1974, edited by Peter Clarke, although *Democracy after the War*, London, Allen and Unwin, 1917, *Problems of a New World*, London, Allen and Unwin, 1921, and *Democracy in a Changing*

Civilisation, London, Bodley Head, 1934, are full of interest. On international issues *Imperialism, a Study*, London, Unwin Hyman, 1988, introduction by J. Townshend, is his best work. The fullest bibliography of Hobson's writing is in A. J. Lee, 'The Social and Political Thought of J. A. Hobson', unpublished Ph.D. thesis, University of London, 1970.

On Hobson

So far there is only one full-scale treatment of Hobson in print, namely, J. Allett, *New Liberalism, The Political Economy of J. A. Hobson*, Toronto, University of Toronto Press, 1981. E. E. Nemmers, *Hobson and Underconsumption*, Amsterdam, North Holland Publishing house, 1956, analyses his positive economic theory. He is given significant coverage in M. Freeden, *The New Liberalism*, Oxford, Clarendon Press, 1978, and *Liberalism Divided*, Oxford, Clarendon Press, 1986; B. Porter, *Critics of Empire*, London, Macmillan, 1968; P. Clarke, *Liberals and Social Democrats*, Cambridge, Cambridge University Press, 1978; N. Etherington, *Theories of Imperialism; War, Conquest and Exploitation*, London, Croom Helm, 1984; D. K. Fieldhouse (ed.) *The Theory of Capitalist Imperialism*, London, Longmans, 1967; J. C. Wood, *Economists and the Empire,* London, Croom Helm, 1983; P. Weiler, *The New Liberalism: Liberal Theory in Great Britain, 1889–1914*, New York, Garland, 1982; P. T. Homan, *Contemporary Economic Thought*, New York, Harper, 1928. As for articles on Hobson, they are becoming fairly plentiful. To single out a reasonable number of them: P. J. Cain, 'J. A. Hobson, Cobdenism, and the Radical Theory of Economic Imperialism', *Economic History Review,* 31 (1978), pp. 565-84; D. J. Coppock, 'A Reconsideration of Hobson's Theory of Unemployment', *Manchester School of Economic and Social Studies*, 21 (1953), pp. 1-21; H. B. Davis, 'Hobson and Human Welfare', *Science and Society*, 1 (1957), pp. 291-318; M. Freeden, 'J. A. Hobson as a New Liberal Theorist:

some aspects of his social thought until 1914', *Journal of the History of Ideas*, 34 (1973), pp. 421-43; D. H. Kruger, 'Hobson, Lenin and Schumpeter on Imperialism', *Journal of the History of Ideas*, 26 (1965), pp. 252-9; T. Lloyd, 'Africa and Hobson's Imperialism', *Past and Present*, no. 55 (1972), pp. 130-53; H. Mitchell, 'Hobson revisited', *Journal of the History of Ideas*, 6 (1965), pp.397-416. Finally, biographical pieces: A. J. Lee, 'J. A. Hobson', in J. M. Bellamy and J. Saville (eds.), *Dictionary of Labour Biography*, London, Macmillan, 1972; R. H. Tawney, 'Hobson, John Atkinson', *Dictionary of National Biography*, 1931-40, pp. 435-6.

Index